DICKENS

on

RAILWAYS

Tony Williams is Associate Editor of *The Dickensian* and a frequent speaker on Dickensian topics. He was President of the International Dickens Fellowship from 2015 to 2017 and has served the Fellowship in various capacities, including as Joint General Secretary from 1999 to 2006, at which time he was also a Trustee of the Charles Dickens Museum in London, where he is now an Honorary Academic Adviser. He is an Honorary Senior Research Fellow in the School of Humanities at the University of Buckingham.

In 2009 he acted as consultant for *Charles Dickens's England*, produced by Guerilla Films, featuring Derek Jacobi. He has co-authored (with Alex Werner) *Dickens's Victorian London*, published in 2011 to accompany the Museum of London's bi-centenary exhibition 'Dickens and London', and recently contributed a chapter on 'Dickens as a Public Figure' to *The Oxford Handbook of Charles Dickens* (2018).

DICKENS

on

RAILWAYS

A Great Novelist's Travels by Train

edited by

TONY WILLIAMS

SAFE HAVEN

First published 2020 by Safe Haven Books Ltd
12 Chinnocks Wharf
14 Narrow Street
London E14 8DJ
www.safehavenbooks.co.uk

A catalogue record for this book
is available from the British Library.

ISBN 978 1 9160453 5 4

1 3 5 7 9 10 8 6 4 2

Typeset in Fournier and Baskerville by M Rules

Printed and bound in the UK by
Clays Ltd, Elcograf, S. p. A.

CONTENTS

LIST OF ILLUSTRATIONS

Dickens straddling the English Channel, *L'Eclipse* magazine, Paris, 14 June 1868 (Granger Historical Picture Archive/Alamy)

'There's Danger on the Line', 1870 (Amoret Tanner/Alamy)

'Charles Dickens relieving the sufferers at the fatal railway accident near Staplehurst', 9 June 1865, *Penny Illustrated Paper*, 24 June 1865 (Album/Alamy)

'At a railway station buffet, a gentleman is offended by the suggestion that he might drink tea . . .', 1875 (Mary Evans Picture Library)

'Professors Ayrton and Perry's new electric railway', 1882, T. P. Collins (© Illustrated London News Ltd/Mary Evans)

'Driver, Stoker at Night', 1889, Paul Hardy (Mary Evans Picture Library)

Introduction

I am never sure of time or place upon a Railroad. I can't read, I can't think, I can't sleep – I can only dream. Rattling along in this railway carriage in a state of luxurious confusion, I take it for granted I am coming from somewhere, and going somewhere else. I seek to know no more. Why things come into my head and fly out again, whence they come and why they come, where they go and why they go, I am incapable of considering. It may be the guard's business, or the railway company's; I only know it is not mine. I know nothing about myself – for anything I know, I may be coming from the Moon.

Disorientation and stimulus to the traveller's imagination are striking features of Charles Dickens's reaction to the new form of transport which developed during his lifetime –recorded here in this extract from an essay in *Household Words* published on 10 May 1856, called 'Railway Dreaming', which continues by exploring his fantasy of 'coming from the Moon'. As this anthology aims to demonstrate, most of Dickens's writing on railways was very much rooted in reality and direct experience, some of it very alarming and dangerous, but always a stimulus to the writer's imagination.

By the time Charles Dickens was eighteen, in 1830, the first piece of railway track had been laid between Manchester and Liverpool, and the railway age had begun. When in March–April 1837 he, with his wife and first child, took possession of their first family house at 48 Doughty Street in Bloomsbury, London, work was going on at nearby Euston on the first mainline railway, from Birmingham, to be brought into the capital. Its first section, from Euston to Boxmoor, was opened on 20 July 1837, a month after Victoria became queen, and the whole line was completed on 17 September 1838.

Dickens's letters of 1838 show us he was already travelling by train. Staying at Llangollen, he wrote to his friend John Forster on 2 November 1838 telling him to 'go straight to Liverpool by the first Birmingham train' (the Grand Junction Railway from Birmingham to Liverpool had been opened in July 1837). On 5 November he wrote from Liverpool to his wife that he would be returning to London with Forster and would arrive 'at the Euston Square Station of the Birmingham Railway.'

By the time of Dickens's death in 1870, most of the main line termini in London had been built. Liverpool Street, Blackfriars and Marylebone were the only ones still to come. Work on St Pancras Station and Gilbert Scott's magnificent Midland Railway Hotel had started in 1868 and was finally declared complete in 1877. In 1863 an Underground Metropolitan Railway had been opened, linking up with King's Cross, which dated from 1852.

Dickens himself was by the late 1850s permanently established at Gad's Hill Place, near Rochester in Kent, but had been commuting up to London from the conveniently nearby Higham Station for some while. He also became a frequent rail traveller in the course of his Reading Tours to all parts of this country and America in the 1850s and 1860s. The Readings created an entirely new way of relating to an audience, enabled him to make full use of his theatrical talents, and allowed his audience to see him face to face as he created his own characters to the life in front of them. He became 'the greatest reader of the greatest writer of the age'.

The initial London season in 1858 ran from April to July, and was followed by a provincial tour, staggering in its extent. By the time it ended in mid-November there had been 100 readings in 42 different towns and cities throughout England, Scotland and Ireland, some of which he visited more than once. The readings took place on one or two evenings and involved a colossal amount of travelling and organisation to fulfil this punishing schedule. Dickens had anticipated the travelling demands, and had contacted railway companies in order to sound them out about concessionary travelling arrangements, but received no positive response.

By 1870 the rail network in this country was well established, and the changes it brought had altered people's lives for ever. Dickens spent his adult life living through those times and recording them.

More than any other technological development, railways characterise the Victorian Age and remain one of its greatest achievements, harnessing natural power and energy by man-made means in the cause of improvement and progress. Dickens was very much a man fascinated by technological progress and its potential for good. John Ruskin described him as being of 'the steam whistle party', a man wedded to the progressive developments of the time. In a letter to his friend, Douglas Jerrold, from Cremona in Italy in November 1844, Dickens is strongly critical of the voices raised in objection to the building of a railway in Venice:

> Instead of going down upon their knees, the drivellers, and thanking Heaven that they live in a time when Iron makes Roads instead of prison bars, and engines for driving screws into the skulls of innocent men.

He often described the act of writing itself as 'getting up steam', and of 'blazing away' when the creative fit was on him.

The pace of life in the nineteenth century was changing fast. If we

think of walking or horse-riding as the pace of life from the Middle
Ages up to the mid-nineteenth century, a good horse-drawn coach
travelling on a well-made road in reasonable weather conditions
could average a speed of 9 to 10 mph: movement as fast as people
envisaged possible up to the 1830s. Between 1839 and 1880 railway
travelling speed increased from 12 mph to 48 mph, averaging about
36 mph for much of the time. By the end of the great railway boom
of the 1840s, over 5,000 miles of track had been laid, and by 1889 this
had increased to 13,000. The railway boom stimulated the economy,
the iron and steel industry especially, and made it easier for goods to
be transported. It gave employment opportunities, very important
at a time when there was much poverty and suffering.

The very real fear of revolution with the Chartist Movement and
the 'Hungry Forties' (and the ever-present memory of the French
Revolution high in the popular consciousness) was somewhat
assuaged by the economic boost given by railway development.
There was the opportunity for speculation, and fortunes could be
made and just as easily lost. Gradually there came about the opportunity to live away from the area where you worked. The landscape
was altered: travellers saw parts of the country they barely knew
existed.

Train travel demanded standardisation of time throughout the
country as 'Greenwich time'. Early timetables gave information
about the conversion of time. For example, the Great Western
Railway timetable for 30 July 1841 notes that 'London time is 4 min
earlier than Reading time, 7.5 min before Cirencester, and 14 min
before Bridgwater.' Great Western directors had demanded standardisation from 1840, but it took until 1852 before the establishment
of telegraph communication along the line enabled transmission of
time signals from London. By the 1880s standardisation had become
pretty much universal.

There were other adjustments to be made. Gentlemen who had
their own horse-drawn carriages would unbridle the horses and

have the carriages fixed to flat trolleys coupled to trains and travel in them, rather than have to share carriages with other people. Guards locked carriage doors to prevent people getting out while the train was moving. In Chapter 40 of *Martin Chuzzlewit*, Dickens has the wonderfully garrulous Mrs Gamp describing the dangers of the shocks and excitement of railway travel for ladies, and the interesting consequences:

> I have heard of one young man, a guard upon a railway, only three year opened ... as is godfather at this present time to six-and-twenty blessed little strangers, equally unexpected, and all on 'em named after the Ingeins as was the cause.

He gives Tony Weller, father of Sam in *Pickwick Papers*, the opportunity to voice several objections to railway travel, from the perspective of a stage coachman, in this extract from *Master Humphrey's Clock* (no. 6 (9 May 1840):

> It wos on the rail, ... I wos a goin' down to Birmingham by the rail, and I wos locked up in a close carriage vith a living widder. Alone we wos; the widder and me wos alone; and I believe it wos only because we WOS alone and there wos no clergyman in the conwayance, that that 'ere widder didn't marry me afore ve reached the half-way station. Ven I think how she began a screaming as we wos a goin' under them tunnels in the dark, – how she kept on a faintin' and ketchin' hold o' me, – and how I tried to bust open the door as was tight-locked and perwented all escape – Ah! It was a awful thing, most awful! ...
>
> And as to the ingein, – a nasty, wheezin', creakin', gaspin', puffin', bustin' monster, alvays out o' breath, with a shiny green-and-gold back, like a unpleasant beetle in that 'ere gas magnifier, – as to the ingein as is alvays a pourin' out red-hot coals at night, and black smoke in the day, the sensiblest thing it

does, in my opinion, is, ven there's somethin' in the vay, and it sets up that 'ere frightful scream vich seems to say, 'Now here's two hundred and forty passengers in the wery greatest extremity o' danger, and here's their two hundred and forty screams in vun!'

This selection of Dickens's writings about railways shows the range of his interests, as traveller, observer, campaigner, enthusiast and one badly shaken by traumatic experience. The Victorians had a very strong sense of theirs as being a new age, an age of progress, the 'summer dawn of time', as Dickens described it in his 'Preliminary Word' to his new journal *Household Words* (see Chapter 1). Speed, excitement, forcing ahead, creating change – all characterise aspects of Dickens's writing and his personality just as much as they characterise the advent of train travel and the prospects it offered.

Through Dickens's words you can share in the at times dislocating experience of a truly new kind of travel, and like him marvel at its potential, lament its destructive capacity, but always be fascinated by it. These pieces also demonstrate Dickens's remarkable range as a writer – novelist, journalist, correspondent, public speaker – and the variety of moods he can be found in: satirical, comic, fearful, angry. In all his writings and guises, he remains (to use a phrase he used in Chapter 12 of *Bleak House*) someone ever sensitive to the 'impress from the moving age'.

Tony Williams
August 2020

1

THE INDIVIDUALITY
OF LOCOMOTIVES

The Railway Dragon

Dickens's journal *Household Words* began weekly publication at the end of March 1850 and continued until May 1859, when it was absorbed into its successor journal, *All the Year Round*. In its first number Dickens, as the 'Conductor' of the magazine, included a 'Preliminary Word' which clearly identifies him as admiring the progressive developments of the time:

> We aspire to live in the Household affections, and to be numbered among the Household thoughts, of our readers. We hope to be the comrade and friend of many thousands of people, of both sexes, and of all ages and conditions, on whose faces we may never look. We seek to bring into innumerable homes, from the stirring world around us, the knowledge of many social wonders, good and evil, that are not calculated to render any of us less ardently persevering in ourselves, less tolerant of one another, less faithful in the progress of mankind, less thankful for the privilege of living in this summer-dawn of time.

He continues to hail the arrival of the new means of transport of his age:

> The mightier inventions of this age are not, to our thinking, all material, but have a kind of souls in their stupendous bodies which may find expression in *Household Words*. The traveller whom we accompany

on his railroad or his steamboat journey, may gain, we hope, some compensation for incidents which these later generations have outlived, in new associations with the Power that bears him onward; with the habitations and the ways of life of crowds of his fellow creatures among whom he passes like the wind; even with the towering chimneys he may see, spirting out fire and smoke upon the prospect.

What is notable here is the way he endows the mechanical creation with a life of its own. Later in the journal's first year of publication, he began to publish occasional paragraphs he called 'Chips' on various aspects of modern life. On 21 September he wrote one on 'The Individuality of Locomotives'.

The Individuality
of Locomotives

I t is a remarkable truth, and, well applied, it might be profitable
to us, in helping us to make fair allowance for the differences
between the temperaments of different men that every Locomotive
Engine running on a Railway, has a distinct individuality and
character of its own. It is perfectly well known to experienced practical engineers, that if a dozen different Locomotive Engines were
made, at the same time, of the same power, for the same purpose,
of like materials, in the same Factory – each of those Locomotive
Engines would come out with its own peculiar whims and ways,
only ascertainable by experience. One engine will take a great meal
of coke and water at once; another will not hear of such a thing, but
will insist on being coaxed by spades-full and buckets-full. One is
disposed to start off, when required, at the top of his speed; another
must have a little time to warm at his work, and to get well into it.
These peculiarities are so accurately mastered by skilful drivers, that
only particular men can persuade particular engines to do their best.
It would seem as if some of these 'excellent monsters' declared, on
being brought out of the stable, 'If it's Smith who is to drive me, I
won't go. If it's my friend Stokes, I am agreeable to anything!' All
Locomotive Engines are low-spirited in damp and foggy weather.
They have a great satisfaction in their work when the air is crisp

and frosty. At such a time they are very cheerful and brisk; but they strongly object to haze and Scotch mists. These are points of character on which they are all united. It is in their peculiarities and varieties of character that they are most remarkable. The Railway Company who should consign all their Locomotives to one uniform standard of treatment, without any allowance for varying shades of character and opinion, would soon fall as much behind-hand in the world as those greater Governments are, and ever will be, who pursue the same course with the finer piece of work called Man.

2

PLANNING A JOURNEY

The first essential requirement for planning a rail journey was a timetable, which in turn required the ability to read and understand such a thing.

Bradshaw's Railway Guide was created by George Bradshaw (1800–53) and published between 1839 and 1961. *Bradshaw's Railway Time Tables and Assistant to Railway Travelling* cost sixpence and was a cloth-bound publication. In 1840 the title was changed to *Bradshaw's Railway Companion*, and the price raised to one shilling, but subsequently it reverted to the original sixpence. A new volume was issued at occasional intervals, and from time to time a supplement kept this up to date. The eight-page edition of 1841 had grown to 32 pages by 1845 and by 1898 to 946 pages, and included maps, illustrations and descriptions of the main features and historic buildings of the towns served by the railways, as well as advertisements for hotels and boarding-houses. There has been a recent upsurge of interest in Bradshaw as a result of several series of television programmes in the UK presented by the former politician Michael Portillo, basing his travels on various versions of Bradshaw's publication.

At times Dickens had found *Bradshaw* confusing and difficult to use, and the complexities of *Bradshaw's Railway Guide* are satirised in 'A Narrative of Extraordinary Suffering', published in *Household Words* on 12 July 1851 and enumerating the miseries caused for one Mr John Lost in attempting to plan a journey to Worcester.

A Narrative of
Extraordinary Suffering

A gentleman of credit and of average ability, whose name we have permission to publish – Mr Lost, of the Maze, Ware – was recently desirous to make a certain journey in England. Previous to entering on this excursion, which we believe had a commercial object (though Mr Lost has for some years retired from business as a Woolstapler, having been succeeded in 1831 by his son who now carries on the firm of Lost and Lost, in the old-established premises at Stratford on Avon, Warwickshire, where it may be interesting to our readers to know that he married, in 1834, a Miss Shakespeare, supposed to be a lineal descendant of the immortal bard), it was necessary that Mr Lost should come to London, to adjust some unsettled accounts with a merchant in the Borough, arising out of a transaction in Hops. His Diary originating on the day previous to his leaving home is before us, and we shall present its rather voluminous information to our readers in a condensed form: endeavouring to extract its essence only.

It would appear that Mrs Lost had a decided objection to her husband's undertaking the journey in question. She observed, 'that he had much better stay at home, and not go and make a fool of himself' – which she seems to have had a strong presentiment that he would ultimately do. A young person in their employ as confidential domestic, also protested against his intention, marking 'that Master warn't the man as was fit for Railways, and Railways warn't the spearses as was fit for Master.' Mr Lost, however, adhering to his purpose, in spite of these dissuasions, Mrs Lost made no effort (as she might easily have done with perfect success) to restrain him by force. But, she stipulated with Mr Lost, that he should purchase an Assurance Ticket of the Railway Passengers' Assurance Company, entitling his representatives to three thousand pounds in case of the worst. It was also understood that in the event of his failing to write home by any single night's post, he would be advertised in *The Times*, at full length, next day.

These satisfactory preliminaries concluded, Mr Lost sent out the confidential domestic (Mary Anne Mag by name, and born of poor but honest parents) to purchase a Railway Guide. This document was the first shock in connexion with his extraordinary journey which Mr Lost and family received. For, on referring to the Index, to ascertain how Ware stood in reference to the Railways of the United Kingdom and the Principality of Wales, they encountered the following mysterious characters:——

WARE TU 6

No farther information could be obtained. They thought of page six, but there was no such page in the book, which had the sportive eccentricity of beginning at page eight. In desperate remembrance of the dark monosyllable TU, they turned to the 'classification of Railways', but found nothing there under the letter T except 'Taff Vale and Aberdare' – and who (as the confidential domestic said) could ever want them! Mr Lost has placed it on record that his 'brain reeled' when he glanced down the page, and found himself, in search of Ware, wandering among such names as Ravenglass, Bootle, and Sprouston.

Reduced to the necessity of proceeding to London by

turnpike-road, Mr Lost made the best of his way to the metropolis in his own one-horse chaise, which he then dismissed in charge of his man, George Flay, who had accompanied him for that purpose. Proceeding to Southwark, he had the satisfaction of finding that the total of his loss upon the Hop transaction did not exceed three hundred and forty-seven pounds, four shillings, and twopence half-penny. This, he justly regarded as, on the whole, a success for an amateur in that promising branch of speculation; in commemoration of his good fortune, he gave a plain but substantial dinner to the Hop Merchant and two friends at Tom's Coffee House on Ludgate Hill.

He did not sleep at that house of entertainment, but repaired in a hackney cab (No. 482) to the Euston Hotel, adjoining the terminus of the North-Western Railway. On the following morning his remarkable adventures may be considered to have commenced.

It appears that with a view to the farther prosecution of his contemplated journey, it was, in the first place, necessary for Mr Lost to make for the ancient city of Worcester. Knowing that place to be attainable by way of Birmingham, he started by the train at eleven o'clock in the forenoon, and proceeded, pleasantly and at an even pace, to Leighton. Here he found, to his great amazement, a powerful black bar drawn across the road, hopelessly impeding his progress!

After some consideration, during which, as he informs us, his 'brain reeled' again, Mr Lost returned to London. Having partaken of some refreshment, and endeavoured to compose his mind with sleep, (from which, however, he describes himself to have derived but little comfort, in consequence of being fitfully pursued by the mystic signs WARE TU 6), he awoke unrefreshed, and at five minutes past five in the afternoon once again set forth in quest of Birmingham. But now, he was even less fortunate than in the morning; for, on arriving at Tring, some ten miles short of his former place of stoppage, he suddenly found the dreaded black barrier across the road, and was thus warned by an insane voice, which seemed to have something supernatural in its awful sound. 'RUGBY TO LEICESTER, NOTTINGHAM, AND DERBY!'

With the spirit of an Englishman, Mr Lost absolutely refused to proceed to either of those towns. If such were the meaning of the voice, it fell powerless upon him. Why should he go to Leicester, Nottingham, and Derby; and what right had Rugby to interfere with him at Tring? He again returned to London, and, fearing that his mind was going, took the precaution of being bled.

When he arose on the following morning, it was with a haggard countenance, on which the most indifferent observer might have seen the traces of a corroding anxiety, and where the practised eye might have easily detected what was really wrong within. Even conscience does not sear like mystery. Where now were the glowing cheek, the double chin, the mellow nose, dancing eye? Fled. And in their place —

In the silent watches of the night, he had formed the resolution of endeavouring to reach the object of his pursuit, by Gloucester, on the Great Western Railway. Leaving London once more, this time at half-an-hour after twelve at noon, he proceeded to Swindon Junction. Not without difficulty. For, at Didcot, he again found the black barrier across the road, and was violently conducted to seven places, with none of which he had the least concern in particular, to one dreadful spot with the savage appellation of Aynho. But, escaping from these hostile towns after undergoing a variety of hardships, he arrived (as has been said) at Swindon Junction.

Here, all hope appeared to desert him. It was evident that the whole country was in a state of barricade, and that the insurgents (whoever they were) had taken their measures but too well. His imprisonment was of the severest kind. Tortures were applied, to induce him to go to Bath, to Bristol, Yatton, Clevedon Junction, Weston- super-Mare Junction, Exeter, Torquay, Plymouth, Falmouth, and the remotest fastnesses of West Cornwall. No chance of Gloucester was held out to him for a moment. Remaining firm, however, and watching his opportunity, he at length escaped more by the aid of good fortune, he considers, than through his own exertions and sliding underneath the dreaded barrier, departed by way of Cheltenham for Gloucester.

And now indeed he might have thought that after combating with so many obstacles, and undergoing perils so extreme, his way at length lay clear before him, and a ray of sunshine fell upon his dismal path. The delusive hope, if any such were entertained by the forlorn man, was soon dispelled. It was his horrible fate to depart from Cirencester exactly an hour before he arrived there, and to leave Gloucester ten minutes before he got to it!

It were vain to endeavour to describe the condition to which Mr Lost was reduced by this overwhelming culmination of his many hardships. It had been no light shock to find his native country in the hands of a nameless foe, cutting off the communication between one town and another, and carrying out a system of barricade, little, if at all, inferior in strength and skill, to the fortification of Gibraltar. It had been no light shock to be addressed by maniac voices urging him to fly to various remote parts of the kingdom. But, this tremendous blow, the annihilation of time, the stupendous reversal of the natural sequence and order of things, was too much for his endurance too much, perhaps, for the endurance of humanity. He quailed beneath it, and became insensible.

When consciousness returned, he found himself again on the North-Western line of Railway, listlessly travelling anywhere. He remembers, he says, Four Ashes, Spread Eagle, and Penkridge. They were black, he thinks, and coaly. He had no business there; he didn't care whether he was there or not. He knew where he wanted to go, and he knew he couldn't go where he wanted. He was taken to Manchester, Bangor, Liverpool, Windermere, Dundee and Montrose, Edinburgh and Glasgow. He repeatedly found himself in the Isle of Man; believes he was, several times, all over Wales; knows he was at Kingstown and Dublin, but has only a general idea how he got there. Once, when he thought he was going his own way at last, he was dropped at a North Staffordshire station called (he thinks in mockery) Mow Cop. As a general rule he observed that whatsoever divergence he made, he came to Edinburgh. But, there were exceptions – as when he was set down on the extreme verge of land at Holyhead, or put aboard a Steamboat, and carried by way of Paris into the heart of France. He thinks the most remarkable journey he was made to take, was from Euston Square into Northamptonshire; so, by the fens of Lincolnshire round to Rugby; thence, through the whole of the North of England and a considerable part of Scotland, to Liverpool; thence, to Douglas in the Isle of Man; and back, by way of Ireland, Wales, Great Yarmouth, and Bishop Stortford, to Windsor Castle. Throughout the whole of these travels, he observed the black-barrier system in active operation, and was always stopped when he least expected it. He invariably travelled against his will, and found a code of cabalistic signs in use all over the country.

Anxiety and disappointment had now produced their natural results. His face was wan, his voice much weakened, his hair scanty and grey, the whole man expressive of fatigue and endurance. It is an affecting instance of the influence of uneasiness and depression on the mind of Mr Lost, that he now commenced wildly to seek the object of his journey in the strangest directions. Abandoning the Railroads on which he had undergone so much, he began to institute a feverish inquiry for it among a host of boarding-houses and hotels. 'Bed, breakfast, boots, and attendance, two and sixpence per day.' – 'Bed and boots, seven shillings per week.' – 'Wines and spirits of the choicest quality.' – 'Night Porter in constant attendance.' – 'For night arrivals, ring the private door bell.' – 'Omnibuses to and from all parts of London, every minute.' – 'Do not confound this house with any other of the same name." Among such addresses to the public, did Mr Lost now seek for a way to Worcester. As he might have anticipated –as he did anticipate in fact, for he was hopeless now – it was not to be found there. His intellect was greatly shaken.

Mr Lost has left, in his Diary, a record so minute of the gradual deadening of his intelligence and benumbing of his faculties, that he can be followed downward, as it were step by step. Thus, we find that when he had exhausted the boarding-houses and hotels, family, commercial and otherwise (in which he found his intellect much enfeebled by the constant recurrence of the hieroglyphic '1 – 6 51 – W. J. A.'), he addressed himself, with the same dismal object, to Messrs Moses and Son, and to Mr Medwin, bootmaker to His Royal Highness Prince Albert. After them, even to inanimate things, as the Patent Compendium Portmanteau, the improved Chaff Machines and Corn Crushers, the Norman Razor, the Bank of England Sealing Wax, Schweppe's Soda Water, the Extract of Sarsaparilla, the Registered Paletot, Rowlands' Kalydor, the Cycloidal Parasol, the Cough Lozenges, the universal night-light, the poncho, Allsopp's pale ale, and the patent knife cleaner. Failing, naturally, in all these appeals, and in a final address to His Grace the Duke of Wellington in the gentlemanly summer garment, and to Mr Burton of the General Furnishing Ironmongery Warehouse, he sank into a stupor, and abandoned hope.

Mr Lost is now a ruin. He is at the Euston Square Hotel. When advised to return home he merely shakes his head and mutters 'Ware Tu . . 6.' No Cabman can be found who will take charge of him on those instructions. He sits continually turning over the leaves of a small, dog's-eared quarto volume with a yellow cover, and babbling in a plaintive voice, 'BRADSHAW, BRADSHAW.'

A few days since, Mrs Lost, having been cautiously made acquainted with his condition, arrived at the hotel, accompanied by the confidential domestic. The first words of the heroic woman were:

'John Lost, don't make a spectacle of yourself, don't. Who am I?'

He replied. 'BRADSHAW.'

'John Lost,' said Mrs Lost, 'I have no patience with you. Where have you been to?'

Fluttering the leaves of the book, he answered, 'To BRADSHAW.'

'Stuff and nonsense, you tiresome man,' said Mrs Lost. 'You put me out of patience. What on earth has brought you to this stupid state?'

He feebly answered, 'BRADSHAW.'

No one knows what he means.

If, unlike Mr Lost, the traveller succeeds in planning a route for his journey, the traveller needs to negotiate the station from which he will undertake it. When Dickens was 'conducting' the second of his weekly journals, *All the Year Round*, he instituted a regular annual Christmas number. The Christmas story for 1866 was *Mugby Junction*, and consisted of a set of short stories written by Dickens and other contributors. Its central character, whose whole working life has been spent with the firm of Barbox Brothers, decides to use the freedom he has in retirement to explore the rail lines connecting with Mugby Junction. What follows here is taken from the introductory part of the story, written by Dickens. Later in this volume, we shall return to *Mugby Junction* for two further examples. Mugby is, of course, Rugby, the great Midland Railway junction station.

Barbox Brothers

'Guard! What place is this?'

'Mugby Junction, sir.'

'A windy place!'

'Yes, it mostly is, sir.'

'And looks comfortless indeed!'

'Yes, it generally does, sir.'

'Is it a rainy night still?'

'Pours, sir.'

'Open the door. I'll get out.'

'You'll have, sir,' said the guard, glistening with drops of wet, and looking at the tearful face of his watch by the light of his lantern as the traveller descended, 'three minutes here.'

'More, I think. – For I am not going on.'

'Thought you had a through ticket, sir?'

'So I have, but I shall sacrifice the rest of it. I want my luggage.'

'Please to come to the van and point it out, sir. Be good enough to look very sharp, sir. Not a moment to spare.'

The guard hurried to the luggage van, and the traveller hurried after him. The guard got into it, and the traveller looked into it.

'Those two large black portmanteaus in the corner where your light shines. Those are mine.'

'Name upon 'em, sir?'

'Barbox Brothers.'

'Who did you say you are?'

'Lamps, sir,' showing an oily cloth in his hand, as farther explanation.

'Surely, surely. Is there any hotel or tavern here?'

'Not exactly here, sir. There is a Refreshment Room here, but –' Lamps, with a mighty serious look, gave his head a warning roll that plainly added – 'but it's a blessed circumstance for you that it's not open.'

'You couldn't recommend it, I see, if it was available?'

'Ask your pardon, sir. If it was –?'

'Open?'

'It ain't my place, as a paid servant of the company, to give my opinion on any of the company's toepics,' – he pronounced it more like toothpicks, –'beyond lamp-ile and cottons,' returned Lamps in a confidential tone; 'but, speaking as a man, I wouldn't recommend my father (if he was to come to life again) to go and try how he'd be treated at the Refreshment Room. Not speaking as a man, no, I would *not*.'

The traveller nodded conviction. 'I suppose I can put up in the town? There is a town here?' For the traveller (though a stay-at-home compared with most travellers) had been, like many others, carried on the steam winds and the iron tides through that Junction before, without having ever, as one might say, gone ashore there.

'Oh, yes, there's a town, sir! Anyways, there's town enough to put up in. But,' following the glance of the other at his luggage, 'this is a very dead time of the night with us, sir. The deadest time. I might a'most call it our deadest and buriedest time.'

'No porters about?'

'Well, sir, you see,' returned Lamps, confidential again, 'they in general goes off with the gas. That's how it is. And they seem to have overlooked you, through your walking to the furder end of the platform. But, in about twelve minutes or so, she may be up.'

'Who may be up?'

'The three forty-two, sir. She goes off in a sidin' till the Up X passes, and then she' – here an air of hopeful vagueness pervaded Lamps – 'does all as lays in her power.'

'I doubt if I comprehend the arrangement.'

'I doubt if anybody do, sir. She's a Parliamentary, sir. And, you see, a Parliamentary, or a Skirmishun –'

'Do you mean an Excursion?'

'That's it, sir. – A Parliamentary or a Skirmishun, she mostly *does* go off into a sidin'. But, when she *can* get a chance, she's whistled out of it, and she's whistled up into doin' all as,' – Lamps again wore the air of a highly sanguine man who hoped for the best, – 'all as lays in her power.'

He then explained that the porters on duty, being required to be in attendance on the Parliamentary matron in question, would doubtless turn up with the gas. In the meantime, if the gentleman would not very much object to the smell of lamp-oil, and would accept the warmth of his little room? – The gentleman, being by this time very cold, instantly closed with the proposal.

A greasy little cabin it was, suggestive, to the sense of smell, of a cabin in a Whaler. But there was a bright fire burning in its rusty grate, and on the floor there stood a wooden stand of newly trimmed and lighted lamps, ready for carriage service. They made a bright show, and their light, and the warmth, accounted for the popularity of the room, as borne witness to by many impressions of velveteen trousers on a form by the fire, and many rounded smears and smudges of stooping velveteen shoulders on the adjacent wall. Various untidy shelves accommodated a quantity of lamps and oil-cans, and also a fragrant collection of what looked like the pocket-handkerchiefs of the whole lamp family.

As Barbox Brothers (so to call the traveller on the warranty of his luggage) took his seat upon the form, and warmed his now ungloved hands at the fire, he glanced aside at a little deal desk, much blotched with ink, which his elbow touched. Upon it were some scraps of coarse paper, and a superannuated steel pen in very reduced and gritty circumstances.

From glancing at the scraps of paper, he turned involuntarily to his host, and said, with some roughness:

'Why, you are never a poet, man?'

Lamps had certainly not the conventional appearance of one, as he stood modestly rubbing his squab nose with a handkerchief so exceedingly oily, that he might have been in the act of mistaking himself for one of his charges. He was a spare man of about the Barbox Brothers time of life, with his features whimsically drawn upward as if they were attracted by the roots of his hair. He had a peculiarly shining transparent complexion, probably occasioned by constant oleaginous application; and his attractive hair, being cut short, and being grizzled, and standing straight up on end as if it in its turn were attracted by some invisible magnet above it, the top of his head was not very unlike a lamp-wick.

'But, to be sure, it's no business of mine,' said Barbox Brothers. 'That was an impertinent observation on my part. Be what you like.

'Some people, sir,' remarked Lamps in a tone of apology, 'are sometimes what they don't like.'

'Nobody knows that better than I do,' sighed the other. 'I have been what I don't like, all my life.'

'When I first took, sir,' resumed Lamps, 'to composing little Comic-Songs-like –'

Barbox Brothers eyed him with great disfavour.

'– To composing little Comic-Songs-like – and what was more hard – to singing 'em afterwards,' said Lamps, 'it went against the grain at that time, it did indeed.'

Something that was not all oil here shining in Lamps's eye, Barbox Brothers withdrew his own a little disconcerted, looked at the fire, and put a foot on the top bar. 'Why did you do it, then?' he asked after a short pause; abruptly enough, but in a softer tone.

'If you didn't want to do it, why did you do it? Where did you sing them? Public-house?'

To which Mr Lamps returned the curious reply: 'Bedside.'

At this moment, while the traveller looked at him for elucidation, Mugby Junction started suddenly, trembled violently, and opened its gas eyes. 'She's got up!' Lamps announced, excited. 'What lays in her power is sometimes more, and sometimes less; but it's laid in her power to get up to-night, by George!'

The legend 'Barbox Brothers', in large white letters on two black surfaces, was very soon afterwards trundling on a truck through a silent street, and, when the owner of the legend had shivered on the pavement half an hour, what time the porter's knocks at the Inn Door knocked up the whole town first, and the Inn last, he groped his way into the close air of a shut-up house, and so groped between the sheets of a shut-up bed that seemed to have been expressly refrigerated for him when last made.

'Let me see. Mugby Junction, Mugby Junction. Where shall I go next? As it came into my head last night when I woke from an uneasy sleep in the carriage and found myself here, I can go anywhere from here. Where shall I go? I'll go and look at the Junction by daylight. There's no hurry, and I may like the look of one Line better than another.'

But there were so many Lines. Gazing down upon them from a bridge at the Junction, it was as if the concentrating Companies formed a great Industrial Exhibition of the works of extraordinary ground spiders that spun iron. And then so many of the Lines went such wonderful ways, so crossing and curving among one another, that the eye lost them. And then some of them appeared to start with the fixed intention of going five hundred miles, and all of a sudden gave it up at an insignificant barrier, or turned off into a workshop. And then others, like intoxicated men, went a little way very straight, and surprisingly slued round and came back again. And then others were so chock-full of trucks of coal, others were so blocked with trucks of casks, others were so gorged with trucks of ballast, others were so set apart for wheeled objects like immense iron cotton-reels: while others were so bright and clear, and others were so delivered over to rust and ashes and idle wheelbarrows out of work, with their legs in the air (looking much like their masters on strike), that there was no beginning, middle, or end to the bewilderment.

Barbox Brothers stood puzzled on the bridge, passing his right hand across the lines on his forehead, which multiplied while he looked down, as if the railway lines were getting themselves photographed on that sensitive plate. Then was heard a distant ringing of bells and blowing of whistles. Then, puppet-looking heads of men popped out of boxes in perspective, and popped in again. Then, prodigious wooden razors, set up on end, began shaving the atmosphere. Then, several locomotive engines in several directions began to scream and be agitated. Then, along one avenue a train came in. Then, along another two trains appeared that didn't come in, but stopped without. Then, bits of trains broke off. Then, a struggling horse became involved with them. Then, the locomotives shared the bits of trains, and ran away with the whole.

3

CHANGING THE
LANDSCAPE

The arrival and progress of the railway caused a great deal of dislocation and change to the landscape. When the ten-year-old Charles Dickens came to London in 1822, he and his family lived at 16 Bayham Street, Camden Town, in north-west London, just north of Euston. At that time it was a semi-rural backwater, but the advent of railway construction was to alter all of that.

The railway that was driven ruthlessly through his neighbourhood, obliterating hundreds of dwellings, originally linked London and Birmingham, so that travellers passing through the Euston Arch that guarded the entrance to Euston Station saw it as the gateway to the rest of the country northwards and to the whole new world being opened up by the railways. The Birmingham terminus was at Curzon Street Station: both the Arch and Curzon Street station were designed by Philip Hardwick.

More recent developments in our own times have seen the development of the West Coast Mainline, connecting the major cities of London, Birmingham, Liverpool and Manchester and Glasgow and, currently, the commencement of construction of HS2, the projected high-speed railway from London to Birmingham and potentially Leeds and Manchester. While the Euston Arch was, scandalously, demolished during the 1960s and is now counted as one of the country's most egregious architectural losses, Curzon Street improbably survived and is to enjoy a new lease of life as the HS2 station for Birmingham.

When Dickens wrote 'Our School' for *Household Words*, published on 11 October 1851, he described revisiting the site of the school, Wellington House Academy, he had attended from 1825 to 1827. The school occupied a site at the junction of Hampstead Road and Granby Terrace. 'We went to look at it, only this last Midsummer,' he wrote,

> and found that the Railway had cut it up root and branch. A great trunk-line had swallowed the playground, sliced away the schoolroom, and pared off the corner of the house: which, thus curtailed of its proportions, presented itself, in a green stage of stucco, profilewise towards the road, like a forlorn flat-iron without a handle, standing on end.

Dickens was to describe the destruction of his childhood hunting ground by the railway twice, first in a polemical piece of non-fiction, 'An Unsettled Neighbourhood', and then in fiction, in a passage in *Dombey and Son*.

An Unsettled Neighbourhood

I t is not my intention to treat of any of those new neighbourhoods which a wise legislature leaves to come into existence just as it may happen; overthrowing the trees, blotting out the face of the country, huddling together labyrinths of odious little streets of vilely constructed houses; heaping ugliness upon ugliness, inconvenience upon inconvenience, dirt upon dirt, and contagion upon contagion. Whenever a few hundreds of thousands of people of the classes most enormously increasing, shall happen to come to the conclusion that they have suffered enough from preventible disease (a moral phenomenon that may occur at any time), the said wise legislature will find itself called to a heavy reckoning. May it emerge from that extremity as agreeably as it slided in. Amen!

No. The unsettled neighbourhood on which I have my eye – in a literal sense, for I live in it, and am looking out of window – cannot be called a new neighbourhood. It has been in existence, how long shall I say? Forty, fifty, years. It touched the outskirts of the fields, within a quarter of a century; at that period it was as shabby, dingy, damp, and mean a neighbourhood, as one would desire not to see. Its poverty was not of the demonstrative order. It shut the street-doors, pulled down the blinds, screened the parlour-windows with the wretched plants in pots, and made a desperate stand to keep up appearances. The genteeler part of the inhabitants, in answering knocks, got behind the door to keep out of sight, and endeavoured to diffuse the fiction that a servant of some sort was the ghostly warder. Lodgings were let, and many more were to let; but, with this exception, signboards and placards were discouraged. A few houses that became afflicted in their lower extremities with eruptions of mangling and clear-starching, were considered a disgrace to the neighbourhood. The working bookbinder with the large door-plate was looked down upon for keeping fowls, who were always going in and out. A corner house with 'Ladies' School' on a board over the first floor windows, was barely tolerated for its educational facilities; and Miss Jamanne the dressmaker, who inhabited two parlours and kept an obsolete work of art representing the Fashions, in the window of the front one, was held at a marked distance by the ladies of the neighbourhood who patronised her, however, with far greater regularity than they paid her.

In those days, the neighbourhood was as quiet and dismal as any neighbourhood about London. Its crazily built houses – the largest, eight-roomed – were rarely shaken by any conveyance heavier than the spring van that came to carry off the goods of a 'sold up' tenant. To be sold up was nothing particular. The whole neighbourhood felt itself liable, at any time, to that common casualty of life. A man used to come into the neighbourhood regularly, delivering the summonses for rates and taxes as if they were circulars. We never paid anything until the last extremity, and Heaven knows how we paid it then. The streets were positively hilly with the inequalities made in them by the man with the pickaxe who cut off the company's supply of water to defaulters. It seemed as if nobody had any money but old Miss Frowze, who lived with her mother at Number Fourteen Little Twig Street, and who was rumoured to be immensely rich; though I don't know why, unless it was that she never went out of doors, and never wore a cap, and never brushed her hair, and was immensely dirty.

As to visitors, we really had no visitors at that time. Stabbers's Band used to come every Monday morning and play for three quarters of

an hour on one particular spot by the Norwich Castle; but how they
first got into a habit of coming, or even how we knew them to be
Stabbers's Band, I am unable to say. It was popular in the neighbourhood, and we used to contribute to it: dropping our halfpence into
an exceedingly hard hat with a warm handkerchief in it, like a sort of
bird's-nest (I am not aware whether it was Mr Stabbers's hat or not),
which came regularly round. They used to open with 'Begone dull
Care!' and to end with a tune which the neighbourhood recognised
as 'I'd rather have a Guinea than a One-pound Note.' I think any
reference to money, that was not a summons or an execution, touched
us melodiously. As to Punches, they knew better than to do anything
but squeak and drum in the neighbourhood, unless a collection was
made in advance – which never succeeded. Conjurors and strong men
strayed among us, at long intervals; but, I never saw the donkey go
up once. Even coster-mongers were shy of us, as a bad job: seeming
to know instinctively that the neighbourhood ran scores with Mrs.
Slaughter, Greengrocer, &c., of Great Twig Street, and consequently
didn't dare to buy a ha'porth elsewhere: or very likely being told so by
young Slaughter, who managed the business, and was always lurking
in the Coal Department, practising Ramo Samee with three potatoes.

As to shops, we had no shops either, worth mentioning. We had
the Norwich Castle, Truman Hanbury and Buxton, by J. Wigzell:
a violent landlord, who was constantly eating in the bar, and constantly coming out with his mouth full and his hat on, to stop his
amiable daughter from giving more credit; and we had Slaughter's;
and we had a jobbing tailor's (in a kitchen), and a toy and hardbake
(in a parlour), and a Bottle Rag Bone Kitchen-stuff and Ladies'
Wardrobe, and a tobacco and weekly paper. We used to run to the
doors and windows to look at a cab, it was such a rare sight; the boys
(we had no end of boys, but where is there any end of boys?) used
to Fly the Garter in the middle of the road; and if ever a man might
have thought a neighbourhood was settled down until it dropped to
pieces, a man might have thought ours was.

What made the fact quite the reverse, and totally changed the neighbourhood? I have known a neighbourhood changed, by many causes, for a time. I have known a miscellaneous vocal concert every evening, do it; I have known a mechanical waxwork with a drum and organ, do it; I have known a Zion Chapel do it; I have known a fireworkmaker's do it; or a murder, or a tallow-melter's. But, in such cases, the neighbourhood has mostly got round again, after a time, to its former character. I ask, what changed our neighbourhood altogether and for ever? I don't mean what knocked down rows of houses, took the whole of Little Twig Street into one immense hotel, substituted endless cab-ranks for Fly the garter, and shook us all day long to our foundations with waggons of heavy goods; but, what put the neighbourhood off its head, and wrought it to that feverish pitch that it has ever since been unable to settle down to any one thing, and will never settle down again? THE RAILROAD has done it all.

That the Railway Terminus springing up in the midst of the neighbourhood should make what I may call a physical change in it, was to be expected. That people who had not sufficient beds for themselves, should immediately begin offering to let beds to the travelling public, was to be expected. That coffee-pots, stale muffins, and egg-cups, should fly into parlour windows like tricks in a pantomime, and that everybody should write up Good Accommodation for Railway Travellers, was to be expected. Even that Miss Frowze should open a cigar-shop, with a what's-his-name that the Brahmins smoke, in the middle of the window, and a thing outside like a Canoe stood on end, with a familiar invitation underneath it, to 'Take a light,' might have been expected. I don't wonder at house-fronts being broken out into shops, and particularly into Railway Dining Rooms, with powdered haunches of mutton, powdered cauliflowers, and great at bunches of rhubarb, in the window. I don't complain of three eight-roomed houses out of every four taking upon themselves to set up as Private Hotels, and putting themselves, as such, into *Bradshaw*, with a charge of so much a day for bed and breakfast, including boot-cleaning and attendance, and so much extra for a private sitting-room – though where the private sitting-rooms can be, in such an establishment, I leave you to judge. I don't make it any ground of objection to Mrs Minderson (who is a most excellent widow woman with a young family) that, in exhibiting one empty soup-tureen with the cover on, she appears to have satisfied her mind that she is fully provisioned as 'The Railway Larder.' I don't point it out as a public evil that all the boys who are left in the neighbourhood, tout to carry carpet bags. The Railway Ham, Beef, and German Sausage Warehouse, I was prepared for. The Railway Pie Shop, I have purchased pastry from. The Railway Hat and Travelling Cap Depot, I knew to be an establishment which in the nature of things must come. The Railway Hair-cutting Saloon, I have been operated upon in; the Railway Ironmongery, Nail and Tool Warehouse; the Railway Bakery; the Railway Oyster Rooms and General Shell Fish Shop; the Railway Medical Hall; and the Railway Hosiery and Travelling Outfitting Establishment; all these I don't complain of. In the same way, I know that the cabmen must and will have beer-shops, on the cellar-flaps of which they can smoke their pipes among the waterman's buckets, and dance the double shuffle. The railway porters must also have their houses of call; and at such places of refreshment I am prepared to find the Railway Double Stout at a gigantic threepence in your own jugs. I don't complain of this; neither do I complain of J. Wigzell having absorbed two houses on each side of him into The Railway Hotel (late Norwich Castle), and setting up an illuminated clock, and a vane at the top of a pole like a little golden Locomotive. But what I do complain of, and what I am distressed at, is, the state of mind – the moral condition – into which the neighbourhood has got. It is unsettled, dissipated, wandering (I believe nomadic is the crack word for that sort of thing just at present), and don't know its own mind for an hour.

I have seen various causes of demoralisation learnedly pointed out in reports and speeches, and charges to grand juries; but, most demoralising thing I know, is Luggage. I have come to the conclusion that the moment Luggage begins to be always shooting about a neighbourhood, that neighbourhood goes out of its mind. Everybody wants to be off somewhere. Everybody does everything in a hurry. Everybody has the strangest ideas of its being vaguely his or her business to go 'down the line'. If any Fast-train could take it, I believe the whole neighbourhood of which I write: bricks, stones, timber, iron-work, and everything else: would set off down the line.

Why, only look at it! What with houses being pulled down and houses being built up, is it possible to imagine a neighbourhood less collected in its intellects? There are not fifty houses of any sort in the whole place that know their own mind a month. Now, a shop says, 'I'll be a toy-shop.' Tomorrow it says, 'No I won't; I'll be a milliner's.' Next week it says, 'No I won't; I'll be a stationer's.' Next week it says, 'No I won't; I'll be a Berlin wool repository.' Take the shop directly opposite my house. Within a year, it has gone through all these changes, and has likewise been a plumber's painter's and glazier's, a tailor's, a broker's, a school, a lecturing-hall, and a feeding-place, 'established to supply the Railway public with a first-rate sandwich and a sparkling glass of Crowley's Alton Ale for threepence.' I have seen the different people enter on these various lines of business, apparently in a sound and healthy state of mind. I have seen them, one after another, go off their heads with looking at the cabs rattling by, top-heavy with luggage, the driver obscured by boxes and portmanteaus crammed between his legs, and piled on the footboard – I say, I have seen them with my own eyes, fired out of their wits by luggage, put up the shutters, and set off down the line.

In the old state of the neighbourhood, if any young party was sent to the Norwich Castle to see what o'clock it was, the solid information would be brought back say, for the sake of argument, twenty minutes to twelve. The smallest child in the neighbourhood who can tell the clock, is now convinced that it hasn't time to say twenty minutes to twelve, but comes back and jerks out, like a little *Bradshaw*, 'Eleven forty.' Eleven forty!

Mentioning the Norwich Castle, reminds me of J. Wigzell. That man is a type of the neighbourhood. He used to wear his shirt-sleeves and his stiff drab trowsers, like any other publican; and if he went out twice in a year, besides going to the Licensed Victuallers' Festival, it was as much as he did. What is the state of that man now? His pantaloons must be railway checks; his upper garment must be a cut-away coat, perfectly undermined by travelling pockets; he must keep a time-bill in his waistcoat besides the two immense ones, UP and DOWN, that are framed in the bar – he must have a macintosh and a railway rug always lying ready on a chair; and he must habitually start off down the line, at five minutes' notice. Now, I know that J. Wigzell has no business down the line; he has no more occasion to go there than a Chinese. The fact is, he stops in the bar until he is rendered perfectly insane by the Luggage he sees flying up and down the street; then, catches up his macintosh and railway rug; goes down the line; gets out at a Common, two miles from a town; eats a dinner at the new little Railway Tavern there, in a choking hurry; comes back again by the next Up-train; and feels that he has done business!

We dream, in this said neighbourhood, of carpet-bags and packages. How can we help it? All night long, when passenger trains are flat, the Goods trains come in, banging and whanging over the turning-plates at the station like the siege of Sebastopol. Then, the mails come in; then, the mail-carts come out; then, the cabs set in for the early parliamentary; then, we are in for it through the rest of the day. Now, I don't complain of the whistle, I say nothing of the smoke and steam, I have got used to the red-hot burning smell from the Breaks which I thought for the first twelvemonth was my own house on fire, and going to burst out; but, my ground of offence is the moral inoculation of the neighbourhood. I am convinced that there is some mysterious sympathy between my hat on my head, and all the hats in hat-boxes that are always going down the line. My shirts and stockings put away in a chest of drawers, want to join the multitude of shirts and stockings that are always rushing everywhere, Express, at the rate of forty mile an hour. The trucks that clatter with such luggage, full trot, up and down the platform, tear into our spirits, and hurry us, and we can't be easy.

In a word, the Railway Terminus Works themselves are a picture of our moral state. They look confused and dissipated, with an air as if they were always up all night, and always giddy. Here, is a vast shed that was not here yesterday, and that may be pulled down to-morrow; there, a wall that is run up until some other building is ready; there, an open piece of ground, which is a quagmire in the middle, bounded on all four sides by a wilderness of houses, pulled down, shored up, broken-headed, crippled, on crutches, knocked about and mangled in all sorts of ways, and billed with fragments of all kinds of ideas. We are, mind and body, an unsettled neigh-bourhood. We are demoralised by the contemplation of luggage in perpetual motion. My conviction is, that you have only to circulate luggage enough – it is a mere question of quantity – through a Quakers' Meeting, and every broad-brimmed hat and slate-coloured bonnet there, will disperse to the four winds at the highest possible existing rate of locomotion.

Always responsive to the tenor of the times, Dickens addresses the impact of the railways most fully in *Dealings with the Firm of Dombey and Son*. Published, as usual for Dickens, in serial instalments, it came out between October 1846 and April 1848, and it is the great novel of the Railway Age.

It is a strikingly contemporary work, coming at a crucial point in Dickens's career, and the novel in which he gives railways a major focus. In it he records social and physical change resulting from railways. In Paul Dombey he creates a capitalist from London whose wealth helped to create the enabling context for the railway boom. He makes Dombey a man of 'about eight and forty years of age', the same age as the new century when this novel was completed. Alongside the social exploration, the novel deals with the personal relationships involved in Dombey's life.

As Dickens' writing career continues after *Dombey and Son*, and railways start to become part of the landscape, they are increasingly assumed into the settings of his novels, so we get occasional references to train travel, but there is no further major exploration of its impact such as we are given in *Dombey and Son*.

Camden Town remains the central subject of these two extracts, where he refers to it as Camberling Town. The particular area whose obliteration he describes becomes Staggs's Gardens. It is an apposite choice of name, since the term 'stag' had come into use during the boom years of railway investment in the 1840s to describe someone who purchased shares in a company with a view to selling them immediately at a profit.

Staggs's Gardens

FROM DOMBEY AND SON, CHAPTER 6

P olly was beset by so many misgivings in the morning, that but for the incessant promptings of her black-eyed companion, she would have abandoned all thoughts of the expedition, and formally petitioned for leave to see number one hundred and forty-seven, under the awful shadow of Mr Dombey's roof. But Susan, who was personally disposed in favour of the excursion, and who (like Tony Lumpkin), if she could bear the disappointments of other people with tolerable fortitude, could not abide to disappoint herself, threw so many ingenious doubts in the way of this second thought, and stimulated the original intention with so many ingenious arguments, that almost as soon as Mr Dombey's stately back was turned, and that gentleman was pursuing his daily road towards the City, his unconscious son was on his way to Staggs's Gardens.

This euphonious locality was situated in a suburb, known by the inhabitants of Staggs's Gardens by the name of Camberling Town; a designation which the Strangers' Map of London, as printed (with a view to pleasant and commodious reference) on pocket handker-chiefs, condenses, with some show of reason, into Camden Town.

The first shock of a great earthquake had, just at that period, rent the whole neighbourhood to its centre. Traces of its course were visible on every side. Houses were knocked down; streets broken through and stopped; deep pits and trenches dug in the ground;

enormous heaps of earth and clay thrown up; buildings that were undermined and shaking, propped by great beams of wood. Here, a chaos of carts, overthrown and jumbled together, lay topsy-turvy at the bottom of a steep unnatural hill; there, confused treasures of iron soaked and rusted in something that had accidentally become a pond. Everywhere were bridges that led nowhere; thoroughfares that were wholly impassable; Babel towers of chimneys, wanting half their height; temporary wooden houses and enclosures, in the most unlikely situations; carcases of ragged tenements, and fragments of unfinished walls and arches, and piles of scaffolding, and wildernesses of bricks, and giant forms of cranes, and tripods straddling above nothing. There were a hundred thousand shapes and substances of incompleteness, wildly mingled out of their places, upside down, burrowing in the earth, aspiring in the air, mouldering in the water, and unintelligible as any dream. Hot springs and fiery eruptions, the usual attendants upon earthquakes, lent their contributions of confusion to the scene. Boiling water hissed and heaved within dilapidated walls; whence, also, the glare and roar of flames came issuing forth; and mounds of ashes blocked up rights of way, and wholly changed the law and custom of the neighbourhood. In short, the yet unfinished and unopened Railroad was in progress; and, from the very core of all this dire disorder, trailed smoothly away, upon its mighty course of civilisation and improvement. But as yet, the neighbourhood was shy to own the Railroad. One or two bold speculators had projected streets; and one had built a little, but had stopped among the mud and ashes to consider farther of it. A bran-new Tavern, redolent of fresh mortar and size, and fronting nothing at all, had taken for its sign The Railway Arms; but that might be rash enterprise – and then it hoped to sell drink to the workmen. So, the Excavators' House of Call had sprung up from a beer-shop; and the old-established Ham and Beef Shop had become the Railway Eating House, with a roast leg of pork daily, through interested motives of a similar immediate and popular description.

Lodging-house keepers were favourable in like manner; and for the like reasons were not to be trusted. The general belief was very slow. There were frowzy fields, and cowhouses, and dunghills, and dustheaps, and ditches, and gardens, and summer-houses, and carpet-beating grounds, at the very door of the Railway. Little tumuli of oyster shells in the oyster season, and of lobster shells in the lobster season, and of broken crockery and faded cabbage leaves in all seasons, encroached upon its high places. Posts, and rails, and old cautions to trespassers, and backs of mean houses, and patches of wretched vegetation, stared it out of countenance. Nothing was the better for it, or thought of being so. If the miserable waste ground lying near it could have laughed, it would have laughed it to scorn, like many of the miserable neighbours. Staggs's Gardens was uncommonly incredulous. It was a little row of houses, with little squalid patches of ground before them, fenced off with old doors, barrel staves, scraps of tarpaulin, and dead bushes; with bottomless tin kettles and exhausted iron fenders, thrust into the gaps. Here, the Staggs's Gardeners trained scarlet beans, kept fowls and rabbits, erected rotten summer-houses (one was an old boat), dried clothes, and smoked pipes. Some were of opinion that Staggs's Gardens derived its name from a deceased capitalist, one Mr Staggs, who had built it for his delectation. Others, who had a natural taste for the country, held that it dated from those rural times when the antlered herd, under the familiar denomination of Staggses, had resorted to its shady precincts. Be this as it may, Staggs's Gardens was regarded by its population as a sacred grove not to be withered by Railroads; and so confident were they generally of its long outliving any such ridiculous inventions, that the master chimney-sweeper at the corner, who was understood to take the lead in the local politics of the Gardens, had publicly declared that on the occasion of the Railroad opening, if ever it did open, two of his boys should ascend the flues of his dwelling, with instructions to hail the failure with derisive cheers from the chimney-pots.

To this unhallowed spot, the very name of which had hitherto been carefully concealed from Mr Dombey by his sister, was little Paul now borne by Fate and Richards.

'That's my house, Susan,' said Polly, pointing it out.

'Is it, indeed, Mrs Richards?' said Susan, condescendingly.

FROM DOMBEY AND SON, CHAPTER 15

Walter had left the fields behind him, and was plodding homeward in the same abstracted mood, when he heard a shout from a man, and then a woman's voice calling to him loudly by name. Turning quickly in his surprise, he saw that a hackney-coach, going in the contrary direction, had stopped at no great distance; that the coach-man was looking back from his box and making signals to him with his whip; and that a young woman inside was leaning out of the window, and beckoning with immense energy. Running up to this coach, he found that the young woman was Miss Nipper, and that Miss Nipper was in such a flutter as to be almost beside herself.

'Staggs's Gardens, Mr Walter!' said Miss Nipper; 'if you please, oh do!'

'Eh?' cried Walter; 'what is the matter?'

'Oh, Mr Walter, Staggs's Gardens, if you please!' said Susan.

'There!' cried the coachman, appealing to Walter, with a sort of exalting despair; 'that's the way the young lady's been a goin' on for up'ards of a mortal hour, and me continivally backing out of no thoroughfares, where she would drive up. I've had a many fares in this coach, first and last, but never such a fare as her.'

'Do you want to go to Staggs's Gardens, Susan?' inquired Walter.

'Ah! She wants to go there! WHERE IS IT?' growled the coachman.

'I don't know where it is!' exclaimed Susan, wildly. 'Mr Walter, I was there once myself, along with Miss Floy and our poor darling

Master Paul, on the very day when you found Miss Floy in the City, for we lost her coming home, Mrs Richards and me, and a mad bull, and Mrs Richards's eldest, and though I went there afterwards, I can't remember where it is, I think it's sunk into the ground. Oh, Mr Walter, don't desert me, Staggs's Gardens, if you please! Miss Floy's darling – all our darlings – little, meek, meek Master Paul! Oh Mr Walter!'

'Good God!' cried Walter. 'Is he very ill?'

'The pretty flower!' cried Susan, wringing her hands, 'has took the fancy that he'd like to see his old nurse, and I've come to bring her to his bedside, Mrs Staggs, of Polly Toodle's Gardens, someone pray!'

Greatly moved by what he heard, and catching Susan's earnestness immediately, Walter, now that he understood the nature of her errand, dashed into it with such ardour that the coachman had enough to do to follow closely as he ran before, inquiring here and there and everywhere, the way to Staggs's Gardens . . .

There was no such place as Staggs's Gardens. It had vanished from the earth. Where the old rotten summer-houses once had stood, palaces now reared their heads, and granite columns of gigantic girth opened a vista to the railway world beyond. The miserable waste ground, where the refuse-matter had been heaped of yore, was swallowed up and gone; and in its frowsy stead were tiers of warehouses, crammed with rich goods and costly merchandise. The old by-streets now swarmed with passengers and vehicles of every kind: the new streets that had stopped disheartened in the mud and waggon-ruts, formed towns within themselves, originating wholesome comforts and conveniences belonging to themselves, and never tried nor thought of until they sprung into existence. Bridges that had led to nothing, led to villas, gardens, churches, healthy public walks. The carcasses of houses, and beginnings of new thoroughfares, had started off upon the line at steam's own speed, and shot away into the country in a monster train. As to the neighbourhood which had hesitated to acknowledge the railroad in its straggling days, that had grown wise and penitent, as any Christian might in such a case, and now boasted of its powerful and prosperous relation. There were railway patterns in its drapers' shops, and railway journals in the windows of its newsmen. There were railway hotels, office-houses, lodging-houses, boarding-houses; railway plans, maps, views, wrappers, bottles, sandwich-boxes, and time-tables; railway hackney-coach and stands; railway omnibuses, railway streets and buildings, railway hangers-on and parasites, and flatterers out of all calculation. There was even railway time observed in clocks, as if the sun itself had given in. Among the vanquished was the master chimney-sweeper, whilom incredulous at Staggs's Gardens, who now lived in a stuccoed house three stories high, and gave himself out, with golden flourishes upon a varnished board, as contractor for the cleansing of railway chimneys by machinery. To and from the heart of this great change, all day and night, throbbing currents rushed and returned incessantly like its life's blood. Crowds of people and mountains of goods, departing and arriving scores upon scores of times in every four-and-twenty hours, produced a fermentation in the place that was always in action. The very houses seemed disposed to pack up and take trips. Wonderful Members of Parliament, who, little more than twenty years before, had made themselves merry with the wild railroad theories of engineers, and given them the live-liest rubs in cross-examination, went down into the north with their watches in their hands, and sent on messages before by the electric telegraph, to say that they were coming. Night and day the conquer-ing engines rumbled at their distant work, or, advancing smoothly to their journey's end, and gliding like tame dragons into the allotted corners grooved out to the inch for their reception, stood bubbling and trembling there, making the walls quake, as if they were dilating with the secret knowledge of great powers yet unsuspected in them, and strong purposes not yet achieved.

But Staggs's Gardens had been cut up root and branch. Oh woe the day when 'not a rood of English ground' – laid out in Staggs's Gardens – is secure!

At last, after much fruitless inquiry, Walter, followed by the coach and Susan, found a man who had once resided in that vanished land, and who was no other than the master sweep before referred to, grown stout, and knocking a double knock at his own door. He knowed Toodle, he said, well. Belonged to the Railroad, didn't he?

'Yes, sir, yes!' cried Susan Nipper from the coach window.

Where did he live now? hastily inquired Walter.

He lived in the Company's own Buildings, second turning to the right, down the yard, cross over, and take the second on the right again. It was number eleven; they couldn't mistake it; but if they did, they had only to ask for Toodle, Engine Fireman, and any one would show them which was his house. At this unexpected stroke of success Susan Nipper dismounted from the coach with all speed, took Walter's arm, and set off at a breathless pace on foot; leaving the coach there to await their return.

4

MAKING A JOURNEY

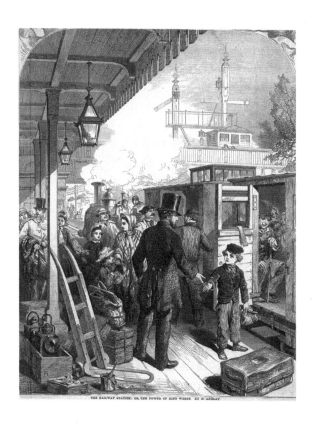

THE RAILWAY STATION; OR, THE POWER OF KIND WORDS. BY H. ANELAY.

In Chapter 20 of *Dombey and* Son, Mr Dombey undertakes a train journey from Euston to Birmingham, accompanied by Major Bagstock. In 1841 this would have taken five hours, reducing to three hours by 1848, the year of the novel's publication. The other major adjustment to be made was the unsettling effect of landscape change and the destruction of whole communities in order to make room for the railway to pass through.

What is so special here, and so new in fiction, is the way Dickens captures the rhythms of the train as it sweeps through the countryside. The language bristles and crackles; the disorientation is exposed; the whirl and vision presented to us in the finest piece of early railway writing. This is published in part seven of the novel, in April 1847, not yet ten years since this particular line opened.

It is also important to note the last part of the piece, as the train enters the Midlands city. Here is a Birmingham industrial landscape Dombey, the capitalist from London whose wealth helped to create the enabling context for the railway boom, would not otherwise know, an industrial world of darkness and misery, a world into which the train has 'let the light of day'. This is again a typical feature of the age: the sources of wealth not known or acknowledged by those who exploit them. Dickens clearly sees the power of progress to make changes for good in people's lives, as well as the inevitable resistance to change and fear of the inhabitants of Staggs's Gardens. The experience is intensified by the way Dickens combines it with an offered moment of human contact, when Toodle, stoker for the train, expresses sympathy to Dombey for his recent loss of his son, Little Paul – and even has the temerity to wear a mourning token.

The Train to Birmingham

FROM CHAPTER 20, DOMBEY AND SON

During the bustle of preparation at the railway, Mr Dombey and the Major walked up and down the platform side by side; the former taciturn and gloomy, and the latter entertaining him, or entertaining himself, with a variety of anecdotes and reminiscences, in most of which Joe Bagstock was the principal performer. Neither of the two observed that in the course of these walks, they attracted the attention of a working man who was standing near the engine, and who touched his hat every time they passed; for Mr Dombey habitually looked over the vulgar herd, not at them; and the Major was looking, at the time, into the core of one of his stories. At length, however, this man stepped before them as they turned round, and pulling his hat off, and keeping it off, ducked his head to Mr Dombey.

'Beg your pardon, Sir,' said the man, 'but I hope you're a doin' pretty well, Sir.'

He was dressed in a canvas suit abundantly besmeared with coal-dust and oil, and had cinders in his whiskers, and a smell of half-slaked ashes all over him. He was not a bad-looking fellow, nor even what could be fairly called a dirty-looking fellow, in spite of this; and, in short, he was Mr Toodle, professionally clothed.

'I shall have the honour of stokin' of you down, Sir,' said Mr Toodle. 'Beg your pardon, Sir. – I hope you find yourself a coming round?'

Mr Dombey looked at him, in return for his tone of interest, as if a man like that would make his very eyesight dirty.

"Scuse the liberty, Sir,' said Toodle, seeing he was not clearly remembered, 'but my wife Polly, as was called Richards in your family –'

A change in Mr Dombey's face, which seemed to express recollection of him, and so it did, but it expressed in a much stronger degree an angry sense of humiliation, stopped Mr Toodle short.

'Your wife wants money, I suppose,' said Mr Dombey, putting his hand in his pocket, and speaking (but that he always did) haughtily.

'No thank'ee, Sir,' returned Toodle, 'I can't say she does. I don't.'

Mr Dombey was stopped short now in his turn: and awkwardly: with his hand in his pocket.

'No, Sir,' said Toodle, turning his oilskin cap round and round; 'we're a doin' pretty well, Sir; we haven't no cause to complain in the worldly way, Sir. We've had four more since then, Sir, but we rubs on.'

Mr Dombey would have rubbed on to his own carriage, though in so doing he had rubbed the stoker underneath the wheels; but his attention was arrested by something in connexion with the cap still going slowly round and round in the man's hand.

'We lost one babby,' observed Toodle, 'there's no denyin'.'

'Lately,' added Mr Dombey, looking at the cap.

'No, Sir, up'ard of three years ago, but all the rest is hearty. And in the matter o' readin', Sir,' said Toodle, ducking again, as if to remind Mr Dombey of what had passed between them on that subject long ago, 'them boys o' mine, they learned me, among 'em, arter all. They've made a wery tolerable scholar of me, Sir, them boys.'

'Come, Major!' said Mr Dombey.

'Beg your pardon, Sir,' resumed Toodle, taking a step before them and deferentially stopping them again, still cap in hand: 'I wouldn't have troubled you with such a pint except as a way of gettin' in the name of my son Biler – christened Robin – him as you was so good as to make a Charitable Grinder on.'

'Well, man,' said Mr Dombey in his severest manner. 'What about him?'

'Why, Sir,' returned Toodle, shaking his head with a face of great anxiety and distress, 'I'm forced to say, Sir, that he's gone wrong.'

'He has gone wrong, has he?' said Mr Dombey, with a hard kind of satisfaction.

'He has fell into bad company, you see, genelmen,' pursued the father, looking wistfully at both, and evidently taking the Major into the conversation with the hope of having his sympathy. 'He has got into bad ways. God send he may come to again, genelmen, but he's on the wrong track now! You could hardly be off hearing of it somehow, Sir,' said Toodle, again addressing Mr Dombey individually; 'and it's better I should out and say my boy's gone rather wrong.'

'Polly's dreadful down about it, genelmen,' said Toodle with the same dejected look, and another appeal to the Major.

'A son of this man's whom I caused to be educated, Major,' said Mr Dombey, giving him his arm. 'The usual return!'

'Take advice from plain old Joe, and never educate that sort of people, Sir,' returned the Major. 'Damme, Sir, it never does! It always fails!'

The simple father was beginning to submit that he hoped his son, the quondam Grinder, huffed and cuffed, and flogged and badged, and taught, as parrots are, by a brute jobbed into his place of schoolmaster with as much fitness for it as a hound, might not have been educated on quite a right plan in some undiscovered respect, when Mr Dombey angrily repeating 'The usual return!' led the Major away. And the Major being heavy to hoist into Mr Dombey's carriage, elevated in mid-air, and having to stop and swear that he would flay the Native alive, and break every bone in his skin, and visit other physical torments upon him, every time he couldn't get his foot on the step, and fell back on that dark exile, had barely time before they started to repeat hoarsely that it would never do: that it always failed: and that if he were to educate 'his own vagabond', he would certainly be hanged.

Mr Dombey assented bitterly; but there was something more in his bitterness, and in his moody way of falling back in the carriage, and looking with knitted brows at the changing objects without, than the failure of that noble educational system administered by the Grinders' Company. He had seen upon the man's rough cap a piece of new crape, and he had assured himself, from his manner and his answers, that he wore it for his son.

So, from high to low, at home or abroad, from Florence in his great house to the coarse churl who was feeding the fire then smoking before them, everyone set up some claim or other to a share in his dead boy, and was a bidder against him! Could he ever forget how that woman had wept over his pillow, and called him her own child! or how he, waking from his sleep, had asked for her, and had raised himself in his bed and brightened when she carne in!

To think of this presumptuous raker among coals and ashes going on before there, with his sign of mourning! To think that he dared to enter, even by a common show like that, into the trial and disappointment of a proud gentleman's secret heart! To think that this lost child, who was to have divided with him his riches, and his projects, and his power, and allied with whom he was to have shut out all the world as with a double door of gold, should have let in such a herd to insult him with their knowledge of his defeated hopes, and their boasts of claiming community of feeling with himself, so far removed: if not of having crept into the place wherein he would have lorded it, alone!

He found no pleasure or relief in the journey. Tortured by these thoughts he carried monotony with him, through the rushing landscape, and hurried headlong, not through a rich and varied country, but a wilderness of blighted plans and gnawing jealousies. The very speed at which the train was whirled along, mocked the swift course of the young life that had been borne away so steadily and so inexorably to its foredoomed end.

The power that forced itself upon its iron way – its own – defiant of all paths and roads, piercing through the heart of every obstacle, and dragging living creatures of all classes, ages, and degrees behind it, was a type of the triumphant monster, Death.

Away, with a shriek, and a roar, and a rattle, from the town, burrowing among the dwellings of men and making the streets hum, flashing out into the meadows for a moment, mining in through the damp earth, booming on in darkness and heavy air, bursting out again into the sunny day so bright and wide; away, with a shriek, and a roar, and a rattle, through the fields, through the woods, through the corn, through the hay, through the chalk, through the mould, through the clay, through the rock, among objects close at hand and almost in the grasp, ever flying from the traveller, and a deceitful distance ever moving slowly within him: like as in the track of the remorseless monster, Death!

Through the hollow, on the height, by the heath, by the orchard, by the park, by the garden, over the canal, across the river, where the sheep are feeding, where the mill is going, where the barge is floating, where the dead are lying, where the factory is smoking, where the stream is running, where the village clusters, where the great cathedral rises, where the bleak moor lies, and the wild breeze smooths or ruffles it at its inconstant will; away, with a shriek, and a roar, and a rattle, and no trace to leave behind but dust and vapour: like as in the track of the remorseless monster, Death!

Breasting the wind and light, the shower and sunshine, away, and still away, it rolls and roars, fierce and rapid, smooth and certain, and great works and massive bridges crossing up above, fall like a beam of shadow an inch broad, upon the eye, and then are lost. Away, and still away, onward and onward ever: glimpses of cottage-homes, of houses, mansions, rich estates, of husbandry and handicraft, of people, of old roads and paths that look deserted, small, and insignificant as they are left behind: and so they do, and what else is there but such glimpses, in the track of the indomitable monster, Death!

Away, with a shriek, and a roar, and a rattle, plunging down into the earth again, and working on in such a storm of energy and perseverance, that amidst the darkness and whirlwind the motion seems reversed, and to tend furiously backward, until a ray of light upon the Wet wall shows its surface flying past like a fierce stream, Away once more into the day, and through the day, with a shrill yell of exultation, roaring, rattling, tearing on, spurning everything with its dark breath, sometimes pausing for a minute where a crowd of faces are, that in a minute more are not; sometimes lapping water greedily, and before the spout at which it drinks has ceased to drip upon the ground, shrieking, roaring, rattling through the purple distance!

Louder and louder yet, it shrieks and cries as it comes tearing on resistless to the goal: and now its way, still like the way of Death, is strewn with ashes thickly. Everything around is blackened. There are dark pools of water, muddy lanes, and miserable habitations far below. There are jagged walls and falling houses close at hand, and through the battered roofs and broken windows, wretched rooms are seen, where want and fever hide themselves in many wretched shapes, while smoke and crowded gables, and distorted chimneys, and deformity of brick and mortar penning up deformity of mind and body, choke the murky distance.

As Mr Dombey looks out of his carriage window, it is never in his thoughts that the monster who has brought him there has let the light of day in on these things: not made or caused them. It was the journey's fitting end, and might have been the end of everything; it was so ruinous and dreary.

5

TRAVELS IN BRITAIN

ARRIVAL OF CHRISTMAS TRAIN, EASTERN COUNTIES RAILWAY.—DRAWN BY DUNCAN.

In 1857 Charles Dickens and his friend the novelist Wilkie Collins, author of the great Victorian detective novels *The Moonstone* and *The Woman in White*, undertook a journey to the north of England, particularly to the Lake District, commencing on 7 September 1857. They subsequently wrote collaboratively about their experiences in five chapters called *The Lazy Tour of Two Idle Apprentices*, published in *Household Words* during October 1857. They adopt the names of Thomas Idle (Collins) and Francis Goodchild (Dickens). There is a substantial amount of writing about the experience of railway travel throughout all five chapters, but this extract, concentrating on the contrasts to be discovered at the 'Junction-Station' of Carlisle, is to be found in the third part, published on 17 October.

From The Lazy Tour of Two Idle Apprentices, *Chapter the Third*

It entered Mr Idle's head, on the borders of Cumberland, that there could be no idler place to stay at, except by snatches of a few minutes each, than a railway station. 'An intermediate station on a line – a junction – anything of that sort', Thomas suggested. Mr Goodchild approved of the idea as eccentric, and they journeyed on and on, until they came to such a station where there was an Inn.

'Here', said Thomas, 'we may be luxuriously lazy; other people will travel for us, as it were, and we shall laugh at their folly.'

It was a Junction-Station, where the wooden razors before mentioned shaved the air very often, and where the sharp electric-telegraph bell was in a very restless condition. All manner of cross-lines of rails came zig-zagging into it, like a Congress of iron vipers; and, a little way out of it, a pointsman in an elevated signal-box was constantly going through the motions of drawing immense quantities of beer at a public-house bar. In one direction, confused perspectives of embankments and arches were to be seen from the platform; in the other, the rails soon disentangled them-selves into two tracks, and shot away under a bridge, and curved round a corner. Sidings were there, in which empty luggage vans and cattle-boxes often butted against each other as if they couldn't agree; and warehouses were there, in which great quantities of goods seemed to have taken the veil (of the consistency of tarpaulin), and to have retired from the world without any hope of getting back to it. Refreshment-rooms were there; one, for the hungry and thirsty Iron Locomotives where their coke and water were ready, and of good quality, for they were dangerous to play tricks with; the other, for the hungry and thirsty human Locomotives, who might take what they could get, and whose chief consolation was provided in the form of three terrific urns or vases of white metal, containing nothing, each forming a breastwork for a defiant and apparently much-injured woman.

Established at this Station, Mr Thomas Idle and Mr Francis Goodchild resolved to enjoy it. But, its contrasts were very violent, and there was also an infection in it.

First, as to its contrasts. They were only two, but they were Lethargy and Madness. The Station was either totally unconscious, or wildly raving. By day, in its unconscious state, it looked as if no life could come to it, as if it were all rust, dust, and ashes – as if the last train for ever, had gone without issuing any Return-Tickets – as if the last Engine had uttered its last shriek and burst. One awkward shave of the air from the wooden razor, and everything changed. Tight office-doors flew open, panels yielded, books, newspapers, travelling-caps and wrappers broke out of brick walls, money chinked, conveyances oppressed by nightmares of luggage came careering into the yard, porters started up from secret places, ditto the much-injured women, the shining bell, who lived in a little tray on stilts by himself, flew into a man's hand and clamoured violently. The pointsman aloft in the signal-box made the motions of drawing, with some difficulty, hogsheads of beer. Down Train! More beer. Up Train! More beer. Cross Junction Train! More beer. Cattle Train! More beer. Goods Train! Simmering, whistling, trembling, rumbling, thundering. Trains on the whole confusion of intersecting rails, crossing one another, bumping one another, hissing one another, backing to go forward, tearing into distance to come close.

People frantic. Exiles seeking restoration to their native carriages, and banished to remoter climes. More beer and more bell. Then, in a minute, the Station relapsed into stupor as the stoker of the Cattle Train, the last to depart, went gliding out of it, wiping the long nose of his oil-can with a dirty pocket- handkerchief.

By night, in its unconscious state, the station was not so much as visible. Something in the air, like an enterprising chemist's established in business on one of the boughs of Jack's beanstalk, was all that could be discerned of it under the stars. In a moment it would break out, a constellation of gas. In another moment, twenty rival chemists, on twenty rival beanstalks, came into existence. Then, the Furies would be seen, waving their lurid torches up and down the confused perspectives of embankments and arches – would be heard, too, wailing and shrieking. Then, the Station would be full of palpitating trains, as in the day; with the heightening difference that they were not so clearly seen as in the day, whereas the station walls, starting forward under the gas, like a hippopotamus's eyes, dazzled the human locomotives with the sauce-bottle, the cheap music, the bedstead, the distorted range of buildings where the patent safes are made, the gentleman in the rain with the registered umbrella, the lady returning from the ball with the registered respirator, and all their other embellishments. And now, the human locomotives, creased as to their countenances and purblind as to their eyes, would swarm forth in a heap, addressing themselves to the mysterious urns and the much-injured women; while the iron locomotives, dripping fire and water, shed their steam about plentifully, making the dull oxen in their cages, with heads depressed, and foam hanging from their mouths as their red looks glanced fearfully at the surrounding terrors, seem as though they had been drinking at half-frozen waters and were hung with icicles. Through the same steam would be caught glimpses of their fellow-travellers, the sheep, getting their white kid faces together, away from the bars, and stuffing the interstices with trembling wool. Also, down among the wheels, of the man with the sledge-hammer, ringing the axles of the fast night-train; against whom the oxen have a misgiving that he is the man with the pole-axe who is to come by-and-bye, and so the nearest of them try to back, and get a purchase for a thrust at him through the bars. Suddenly, the bell would ring, the steam would stop with one hiss and a yell, the chemists on the beanstalks would be busy, the avenging Furies would bestir themselves, the fast night-train would melt from eye and ear, the other trains going their ways more slowly would be heard faintly rattling in the distance like old-fashioned watches running down, the sauce-bottle and cheap music retired from view, even the bedstead went to bed, and there was no such visible thing as the Station to vex the cool wind in its blowing, or perhaps the autumn lightning, as it found out the iron rails.

The infection of the Station was this: — When it was in its raving state, the Apprentices found it impossible to be there, without labouring under the delusion that they were in a hurry. To Mr Goodchild, whose ideas of idleness were so imperfect, this was no unpleasant hallucination, and accordingly that gentleman went through great exertions in yielding to it, and running up and down the platform, jostling everybody, under the impression that he had a highly important mission somewhere, and had not a moment to lose. But, to Thomas Idle, this contagion was so very unacceptable an incident of the situation, that he struck on the fourth day, and requested to be moved.

'This place fills me with a dreadful sensation,' said Thomas, 'of having something to do. Remove me, Francis.'

'Where would you like to go next?' was the question of the ever-engaging Goodchild.

'I have heard there is a good old Inn at Lancaster, established in a fine old house: an Inn where they give you Bride-cake every day after dinner,' said Thomas Idle. 'Let us eat Bridecake without the trouble of being married, or of knowing anybody in that ridiculous dilemma.'

Mr Goodchild, with a lover's sigh, assented. They departed from the Station in a violent hurry (for which, it is unnecessary to observe, there was not the least occasion), and were delivered at the fine old house at Lancaster, on the same night.

On 27, 29 and 30 December 1853 Dickens gave his first Public Readings in Birmingham Town Hall, in order to support the recently established Literary and Scientific Institute, later to become the Birmingham and Midland Institute. He read from *A Christmas Carol* on 27 and 30 and *The Cricket on the Hearth* on 29 December. Keen as always to see what else might be obtained from this visit, he used his free day on 28 December to take the train to Wolverhampton. There had been a heavy snowstorm at the start of his visit to the area.

'Fire and Snow' was published in *Household Words* on 21 January 1854 and is included here in its entirety.

Fire and Snow

C an this be the region of cinders and coal-dust, which we have traversed before now, divers times, both by night and by day, when the dirty wind rattled as it came against us charged with fine particles of coal, and the natural colour of the earth and all its vegetation might have been black, for anything our eyes could see to the contrary in a waste of many miles? Indeed it is the same country, though so altered that on this present day when the old year is near its last, the North-East wind blows white, and all the ground is white pure white insomuch that if our lives depended on our identifying a mound of ashes as we jar along this Birmingham and Wolverhampton Railway, we could not find a handful.

The sun shines brightly, though it is a cold cold sun, this piercing day; and when the Birmingham tunnel disgorges us into the frosty air, we find the pointsman housed in no mere box, but in a resplendent pavilion, all bejewelled with dazzling icicles, the least a yard long. A radiant pointsman he should be, we think, invested by fairies with a dress of rainbow hues, and going round and round in some gorgeously playful manner on a gold and silver pivot. But, he has changed neither his stout great coat, nor his stiff hat, nor his stiff attitude of watch; and as (like the ghostly dagger of Macbeth) he marshals us the way that we were going, we observe him to be a mortal with a red face – red, in part from a seasonable joviality of spirit, and in part from frost and wind with the encrusted snow dropping silently off his outstretched arm.

Redder than ever are the very red-brick little houses outside Birmingham all staring at the railway in the snowy weather, like plethoric old men with white heads. Clean linen drying in yards seems ill-washed, against the intense white of the landscape. Far and near, the tall tall chimneys look out over one another's shoulders for the swart ashes familiar to them, and can discern nothing but snow. Is this the smoke of other chimneys setting in so heavily from the north-east, and overclouding the short brightness of the day? No. By the North Pole it is more snow!

Making directly at us, and flying almost horizontally before the wind, it rushes against the train, in a dark blast profusely speckled as it were with drifting white feathers. A sharp collision, though a harmless one! No wonder that the engine seems to have a fearful cold in his head. No wonder, with a deal of out-door work in such a winter, that he is very hoarse and very short of breath, very much blown when we come to the next station, and very much given to weeping, snorting and spitting, all the time he stops!

Which is short enough, for these little upstairs stations at the tops of high arches, whence we almost look down the chimneys of scattered workshops, and quite inhale their smoke as it comes puffing at us – these little upstairs stations rarely seem to do much business anywhere, and just now are like suicidal heights to dive from into depths of snow. So, away again over the moor, where the clanking serpents usually writhing above coal-pits, are dormant and whitened over – this being holiday time – but where those grave monsters, the blast-furnaces, which cannot stoop to recreation, are awake and roaring. Now, a smoky village; now, a chimney; now, a dormant serpent who seems to have been benumbed in the act of working his way for shelter into the lonely little engine-house by the pit's mouth; now, a pond with black specks sliding and skating; now, a drift with similar specks half sunken in it throwing snowballs; now, a cold white altar of snow with fire blazing on it; now, a dreary open space of mound and fell, snowed smoothly over, and closed in at last by sullen cities of chimneys. Not altogether agreeable to think of crossing such space without a guide, and being swallowed by a long-abandoned, long- forgotten shaft. Not even agreeable, in this undermined country, to think of half-a-dozen railway arches with the train upon them, suddenly vanishing through the snow into the excavated depths of a coal-forest.

Snow, wind, ice, and Wolverhampton – all together. No carriage at the station, everything snowed up. So much the better. The Swan will take us under its warm wing, walking or riding. Where is the Swan's nest? In the market-place. So much the better yet, for it is market-day, and there will be something to see from the Swan's nest.

Up the streets of Wolverhampton, where the doctor's bright door-plate is dimmed as if Old Winter's breath were on it, and the lawyer's office window is appropriately misty, to the market-place: where we find a cheerful bustle and plenty of people – for the most part pretending not to like the snow, but liking it very much, as people generally do. The Swan is a bird of a good substantial brood, worthy to be a country cousin of the hospitable Hen and Chickens, whose company we have deserted for only a few hours and with whom we shall roost again at Birmingham to-night. The Swan has bountiful coal-country notions of firing, snug homely rooms, cheerful windows looking down upon the clusters of snowy umbrellas in the market-place, and on the chaffering and chattering which is pleasantly hushed by the thick white down lying so deep, and softly falling still. Neat bright-eyed waitresses do the honours of the Swan. The Swan is confident about its soup, is troubled with no distrust concerning codfish, speaks the word of promise in relation to an enormous chine of roast beef, one of the dishes at 'the Ironmasters' dinner', which will be disengaged at four. The Ironmasters' dinner! It has an imposing sound. We think of the Ironmasters joking, drinking to their Iron mistresses, clinking their glasses with a metallic ring, and comporting themselves at the festive board with the might of men who have mastered iron.

Now for a walk! Not in the direction of the furnaces, which we will see to-night when darkness shall set off the fires; but in the country, with our faces towards Wales. Say, ye hoary finger-posts whereon the name of picturesque old Shrewsbury is written in characters of frost; ye hedges lately bare, that have burst into snowy foliage; ye glittering trees, from which the wind blows sparkling dust; ye high drifts by the roadside, which are blue a-top, where ye are seen opposed to the bright red and yellow of the horizon; say all of ye, is summer the only sea-son for enjoyable walks! Answer, roguish crow, alighting on a sheep's back to pluck his wool off for an extra blanket, and skimming away, so black, over the white field; give us your opinion, swinging ale-house signs, and cosey little bars; speak out, farrier's shed with faces all a-glow, fountain of sparks, heaving bellows, and ringing music; tell us, cottage hearths and sprigs of holly in cottage windows; be eloquent in praise of wintry walks, you sudden blasts of wind that pass like shiverings of Nature, you deep roads, you solid fragments of old hayricks with your fragrance frozen in! Even you, drivers of toiling carts, coal-laden, keeping company together behind your charges, dog-attended and basket- bearing: even you, though it is no easy work to stop, every now and then, and chip the snow away from the clogged wheels with picks, will have a fair word to say for winter, will you not!

Down to the solitary factory in the dip of the road, deserted of holiday-makers, and where the water-mill is frozen up then turn. As we draw nigh to our bright bird again, the early evening is closing in, the cold increases, the snow deadens and darkens, and lights spring up in the shops. A wet walk, ankle deep in snow the whole way. We must buy some stockings, and borrow the Swan's slippers before dinner.

It is a mercy that we step into the toyshop to buy a pocket-comb too, or the pretty child- customer (as it seems to us, the only other customer the elderly lady of the toyshop has lately had), might have stood divided between the two puzzles at one shilling each, until the

putting up of the shutters. But, the incursion of our fiery faces and
snowy dresses, coupled with our own individual recommendation
of the puzzle on the right hand, happily turn the scale. The best
of pocket-combs for a shilling, and now for the stockings. Dibbs
'don't keep 'em', though he writes up that he does, and Jibbs is so
beleaguered by country people making market-day and Christmas-
week purchases, that his shop is choked to the pavement. Mibbs is
the man for our money, and Mibbs keeps everything in the stocking
line, though he may not exactly know where to find it. However, he
finds what we want, in an inaccessible place, after going up ladders
for it like a lamplighter; and a very good article it is, and a very
civil worthy trader Mibbs is, and may Mibbs increase and multiply!
Likewise young Mibbs, unacquainted with the price of anything in
stock, and young Mibbs's aunt who attends to the ladies' department.

The Swan is rich in slippers in those good old flip-flap inn slippers
which nobody can keep on, which knock double knocks on every
stair as their wearer comes down stairs, and fly away over the ban-
isters before they have brought him to level ground. Rich also is the
Swan in wholesome well-cooked dinner, and in tender chine of beef,
so brave in size that the mining of all the powerful Ironmasters is but
a sufficient outlet for its gravy. Rich in things wholesome and sound
and unpretending is the Swan, except that we would recommend the
good bird not to dip its beak into its sherry. Under the change from
snow and wind to hot soup, drawn red curtains, fire and candle, we
observe our demonstrations at first to be very like the engine's at
the little station; but they subside, and we dine vigorously –another
tribute to a winter walk! – and finding that the Swan's ideas of something hot to drink are just and laudable, we adopt the same, with
emendations (in the matter of lemon chiefly) of which modesty and
total abstinence principles forbid the record. Then, thinking drows-
ily and delightfully of all things that have occurred to us during the
last four-and-twenty hours, and of most things that have occurred
to us during the last four-and-twenty years, we sit in arm chairs,

amiably basking before the fire – playthings for infancy – creatures to be asked a favour of – until aroused by the fragrance of hot tea and muffins. These we have ordered, principally as a perfume.

The bill of the Swan is to be commended as not out of proportion to its plumage; and now, our walking shoes being dried and baked, we must get them on somehow – for the rosy driver with his carriage and pair who is to take us among the fires on the blasted heath by Bilston announces from under a few shawls, and the collars of three or four coats, that we must be going. Away we go, obedient to the summons, and, having taken leave of the lady in the Swan's bar opposite the door, who is almost rustled out of her glass case and blown up stairs whenever the door opens, we are presently in outer darkness grinding the snow.

Soon the fires begin to appear. In all this ashy country, there is still not a cinder visible; in all this land of smoke, not a stain upon the universal white. A very novel and curious sight is presented by the hundreds of great fires blazing in the midst of the cold dead snow. They illuminate it very little. Sometimes, the construction of a furnace, kiln, or chimney, admits of a tinge being thrown upon the pale ground near it; but, generally the fire burns in its own sullen ferocity, and the snow lies impassive and untouched. There is a glare in the sky, flickering now and then over the greater furnaces, but the earth lies stiff in its winding sheet, and the huge corpse candles burning above it affect it no more than colossal tapers of state move dead humanity.

Sacrificial altars, varying in size, but all gigantic, and all made of ice and snow, abound. Tongues of flame shoot up from them, and pillars of fire turn and twist upon them. Fortresses on fire, a whole town in a blaze; Moscow newly kindled, we see fifty times; rattling and crashing noises strike the ear, and the wind is loud. Thus, crushing the snow with our wheels, and sidling over hillocks of it, and sinking into drifts of it, we roll on softly through a forest of conflagration; the rosy-faced driver, concerned for the honour of his locality, much regretting that many fires are making holiday to-night, and that we see so few.

Come we at last to the precipitous wooden steps by which we are to be mast-headed at a railway station. Good night to rosy-face, the cheeriest man we know, and up. Station very gritty as a general characteristic. Station very dark, the gas being frozen. Station very cold, as any timber cabin suspended in the air with such a wind making lunges at it, would be. Station very dreary, being a station. Man and boy behind money-taking partition, checking accounts, and not able to unravel a knot of seven and sixpence. Small boy with a large package on his back, like Christian with his bundle of sins, sent down into the snow an indefinite depth and distance, with instructions to 'look sharp in delivering that, and then cut away back here for another.' Second small boy in search of basket for Mr. Brown, unable to believe that it is not there, and that anybody can have dared to disappoint Brown. Six third-class passengers prowling about, and trying in the dim light of one oil lamp to read with interest the dismal time-bills and notices about throwing stones at trains, upon the walls. Two more, scorching themselves at the rusty stove. Shivering porter going in and out, bell in hand, to look for the train, which is overdue, finally gives it up for the present, and puts down the bell – also the spirits of the passengers. In our own innocence we repeatedly mistake the roaring of the nearest furnace for the approach of the train, run out, and return covered with ignominy. Train in sight at last – but the other train – which don't stop here – and it seems to tear the trembling station limb from limb, as it rushes through. Finally, some half-an-hour behind its time through the tussle it has had with the snow, comes our expected engine, shrieking with indignation and grief. And as we pull the clean white coverlid over us in bed at Birmingham, we think of the whiteness lying on the broad landscape all around for many a frosty windy mile, and find that it makes bed very comfortable.

6

TRAVELS IN AMERICA

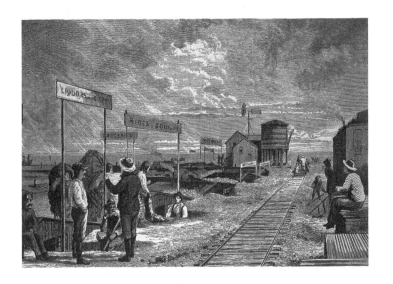

Dickens visited America twice, once from 22 January to 7 June 1842, including crossing into Canada, where he stayed for nearly a month, and once from 19 November 1867 to 22 April 1868, with a briefer visit to Canada.

The 1867–8 visit was principally a public reading tour. The 1842 visit came about as the result of invitations from Dickens's American friends, and reflected his excitement at the prospect of visiting a new and independent republic which appeared to echo his own radical sentiments. For Americans, there was the prospect of seeing this new and rising British literary phenomenon. With such high expectations on both sides, the reality was bound to be a disappointment. America proved not to be 'the republic of (Dickens's) imagination'. He was particularly repulsed by what he saw of slavery.

There were three kinds of writing which emerged from the 1842 visit. Dickens maintained an extensive correspondence with friends at home during these visits, and drew on these letters when he turned his experiences into published works, in *American Notes for General Circulation* in 1842 and in the chapters in *Martin Chuzzlewit* devoted to Martin and Mark Tapley's experiences during their visit to America.

Two extracts are provided here, both from the earlier visit. An account of Dickens's travels during the later visit may be found in George Dolby's memoir of his years as his reading tours manager, published in 1885 as *Charles Dickens As I Knew Him*. In Chapter 7 Dolby writes about travelling by rail with Dickens in America in December 1867:

On Saturday, December 7th, we left our kind friends in Boston for our first railway journey to New York, and great was the crowd to say 'good-bye' to the one they all loved so dearly. The journey was undertaken by the Shore Line Route, the most convenient as to the hours of departure in the morning, a matter to be thought of when it is considered the distance from Boston to New York is about 240 miles, and the time occupied in performing this journey (by express train) is nine hours. This time would be considerably reduced if the train had not to cross two wide rivers, one at Stonnington and the other at New London, this causing a delay of certainly one hour on the journey: although everything is done to make the inconvenience as light as possible, by running the train on to the ferry boat (in which is an excellent restaurant), and conveying it across the river bodily, without troubling the passengers to move from their seats, unless they wish to do so.

A later work related to this visit is *A Child's Journey with Dickens* (1912) by Kate Douglas Wiggin, who in 1903 wrote *Rebecca of Sunnybrook Farm*. Dickens had been giving a public reading in Portland on 30 March 1868 and was travelling to Boston by train (the day after the President, Andrew Johnson, had been formally impeached, she notes) when she saw him.

When the train stopped for two or three minutes at North Berwick, the people on the side of the car next the station suddenly arose and looked eagerly out at some object of apparent interest. I was not, at any age, a person to sit still in her seat when others were looking out of windows, and my small nose was quickly flattened against one of the panes. There on the platform stood the Adored One! His hands were plunged deep in his pockets (a favourite gesture), but presently one was removed to wave away laughingly a piece of the famous Berwick sponge cake, offered him by Mr Osgood, of Boston, his travelling companion and friend.

I knew him at once! – the smiling, genial, mobile face, rather highly coloured, the brilliant eyes, the watch chain, the red carnation in the button-hole, and the expressive hands, much given to gesture. It was only a momentary view, for the train started, and Dickens vanished, to resume his place in the car next to ours, where he had been, had I known it, ever since we left Portland.

When my mother was again occupied with her book, I slipped away and entered the next car. I took a humble, unoccupied seat near the end, close by the much patronised tank of (unsterilised) drinking-water, and the train-boy's basket of popcorn balls and molasses candy, and gazed steadily at the famous man, who was chatting busily with Mr. Osgood.

Subsequently they had a substantial conversation.

An American Railroad: Lowell and its Factory System

AMERICAN NOTES (1842), CHAPTER 4

B efore leaving Boston, I devoted one day to an excursion to Lowell. I assign a separate chapter to this visit; not because I am about to describe it at any great length, but because I remember it as a thing by itself, and am desirous that my readers should do the same.

I made acquaintance with an American railroad, on this occasion, for the first time. As these works are pretty much alike all through the States, their general characteristics are easily described.

There are no first and second class carriages as with us; but there is a gentleman's car and a ladies' car: the main distinction between which is that in the first, everybody smokes; and in the second, nobody does. As a black man never travels with a white one, there is also a negro car; which is a great, blundering, clumsy chest, such as Gulliver put to sea in, from the kingdom of Brobdingnag. There is a great deal of jolting, a great deal of noise, a great deal of wall, not much window, a locomotive engine, a shriek, and a bell.

The cars are like shabby omnibuses, but larger: holding thirty, forty, fifty, people. The seats, instead of stretching from end to end, are placed crosswise. Each seat holds two persons. There is a long row of them on each side of the caravan, a narrow passage up the middle, and a door at both ends. In the centre of the carriage there is usually a stove, fed with charcoal or anthracite coal; which is for the most part red-hot. It is insufferably close; and you see the hot air fluttering between yourself and any other object you may happen to look at, like the ghost of smoke.

In the ladies' car, there are a great many gentlemen who have ladies with them. There are also a great many ladies who have nobody with them: for any lady may travel alone, from one end of the United States to the other, and be certain of the most courteous and considerate treatment everywhere. The conductor or check-taker, or guard, or whatever he may be, wears no uniform. He walks up and down the car, and in and out of it, as his fancy dictates; leans against the door with his hands in his pockets and stares at you, if you chance to be a stranger; or enters into conversation with the passengers about him. A great many newspapers are pulled out, and a few of them are read. Everybody talks to you, or to anybody else who hits his fancy. If you are an Englishman, he expects that that railroad is pretty much like an English railroad. If you say 'No', he says 'Yes?' (interrogatively), and asks in what respect they differ. You enumerate the heads of difference, one by one, and he says 'Yes?' (still interrogatively) to each. Then he guesses that you don't travel faster in England; and on your replying that you do, says 'Yes?' again (still interrogatively), and it is quite evident, don't believe it. After a long pause he remarks, partly to you, and partly to the knob on the top of his stick, that 'Yankees are reckoned to be considerable of a go-ahead people too;' upon which YOU say 'Yes', and then HE says 'Yes' again (affirmatively this time); and upon your looking out of window, tells you that behind that hill, and some three miles from the next station, there is a clever town in a smart lo-ca-tion, where he expects you have concluded to stop. Your answer in the negative naturally leads to more questions in reference to your intended route (always pronounced rout); and wherever you are going, you invariably learn that you can't get there without immense difficulty and danger, and that all the great sights are somewhere else.

If a lady take a fancy to any male passenger's seat, the gentleman who accompanies her gives him notice of the fact, and he immediately vacates it with great politeness. Politics are much discussed, so are banks, so is cotton.

Quiet people avoid the question of the Presidency, for there will be a new election in three years and a half, and party feeling runs very high: the great constitutional feature of this institution being, that directly the acrimony of the last election is over, the acrimony of the next one begins; which is an unspeakable comfort to all strong politicians and true lovers of their country: that is to say, to ninety-nine men and boys out of every ninety-nine and a quarter.

Except when a branch road joins the main one, there is seldom more than one track of rails; so that the road is very narrow, and the view, where there is a deep cutting, by no means extensive. When there is not, the character of the scenery is always the same. Mile after mile of stunted trees: some hewn down by the axe, some blown down by the wind, some half fallen and resting on their neighbours, many mere logs half hidden in the swamp, others mouldered away to spongy chips. The very soil of the earth is made up of minute fragments such as these; each pool of stagnant water has its crust of vegetable rottenness; on every side there are the boughs, and trunks, and stumps of trees, in every possible stage of decay, decomposition, and neglect. Now you emerge for a few brief minutes on an open country, glittering with some bright lake or pool, broad as many an English river, but so small here that it scarcely has a name; now catch hasty glimpses of a distant town, with its clean white houses and their cool piazzas, its prim New England church and school-house; when whir-r-r-r! almost before you have seen them, comes the same dark screen: the stunted trees, the stumps, the logs, the stagnant water – all so like the last that you seem to have been transported back again by magic.

The train calls at stations in the woods, where the wild impossibility of anybody having the smallest reason to get out, is only to

be equalled by the apparently desperate hopelessness of there being
anybody to get in. It rushes across the turnpike road, where there
is no gate, no policeman, no signal: nothing but a rough wooden
arch, on which is painted 'WHEN THE BELL RINGS, LOOK
OUT FOR THE LOCOMOTIVE.' On it whirls headlong, dives
through the woods again, emerges in the light, clatters over frail
arches, rumbles upon the heavy ground, shoots beneath a wooden
bridge which intercepts the light for a second like a wink, suddenly
awakens all the slumbering echoes in the main street of a large town,
and dashes on haphazard, pell-mell, neck-or-nothing, down the
middle of the road. There – with mechanics working at their trades,
and people leaning from their doors and windows, and boys flying
kites and playing marbles, and men smoking, and women talking,
and children crawling, and pigs burrowing, and unaccustomed
horses plunging and rearing, close to the very rails – there – on, on,
on – tears the mad dragon of an engine with its train of cars; scattering in all directions a shower of burning sparks from its wood fire;
screeching, hissing, yelling, panting; until at last the thirsty monster
stops beneath a covered way to drink, the people cluster round, and
you have time to breathe again.

I was met at the station at Lowell by a gentleman intimately
connected with the management of the factories there; and gladly
putting myself under his guidance, drove off at once to that quarter
of the town in which the works, the object of my visit, were situated.

Although only just of age – for if my recollection serve me, it has
been a manufacturing town barely one-and-twenty years – Lowell
is a large, populous, thriving place. Those indications of its youth
which first attract the eye, give it a quaintness and oddity of character which, to a visitor from the old country, is amusing enough.
It was a very dirty winter's day, and nothing in the whole town
looked old to me, except the mud, which in some parts was almost
knee-deep, and might have been deposited there, on the subsiding
of the waters after the Deluge. In one place, there was a new wooden

church, which, having no steeple, and being yet unpainted, looked like an enormous packing-case without any direction upon it. In another there was a large hotel, whose walls and colonnades were so crisp, and thin, and slight, that it had exactly the appearance of being built with cards. I was careful not to draw my breath as we passed, and trembled when I saw a workman come out upon the roof, lest with one thoughtless stamp of his foot he should crush the structure beneath him, and bring it rattling down. The very river that moves the machinery in the mills (for they are all worked by water power), seems to acquire a new character from the fresh buildings of bright red brick and painted wood among which it takes its course; and to be as light- headed, thoughtless, and brisk a young river, in its murmurings and tumblings, as one would desire to see. One would swear that every 'Bakery', 'Grocery', and 'Bookbindery', and other kind of store, took its shutters down for the first time, and started in business yesterday. The golden pestles and mortars fixed as signs upon the sun-blind frames outside the Druggists', appear to have been just turned out of the United States' Mint; and when I saw a baby of some week or ten days old in a woman's arms at a street corner, I found myself unconsciously wondering where it came from: never supposing for an instant that it could have been born in such a young town as that.

There are several factories in Lowell, each of which belongs to what we should term a Company of Proprietors, but what they call in America a Corporation. I went over several of these; such as a woollen factory, a carpet factory, and a cotton factory: examined them in every part; and saw them in their ordinary working aspect, with no preparation of any kind, or departure from their ordinary everyday proceedings. I may add that I am well acquainted with our manufacturing towns in England, and have visited many mills in Manchester and elsewhere in the same manner.

I happened to arrive at the first factory just as the dinner hour was over, and the girls were returning to their work; indeed the stairs of the mill were thronged with them as I ascended. They were all well dressed, but not to my thinking above their condition; for I like to see the humbler classes of society careful of their dress and appearance, and even, if they please, decorated with such little trinkets as come within the compass of their means.

Supposing it confined within reasonable limits, I would always encourage this kind of pride, as a worthy element of self- respect, in any person I employed; and should no more be deterred from doing so, because some wretched female referred her fall to a love of dress, than I would allow my construction of the real intent and meaning of the Sabbath to be influenced by any warning to the well-disposed, founded on his backslidings on that particular day, which might emanate from the rather doubtful authority of a murderer in Newgate.

These girls, as I have said, were all well dressed: and that phrase necessarily includes extreme cleanliness. They had serviceable bonnets, good warm cloaks, and shawls; and were not above clogs and pattens. Moreover, there were places in the mill in which they could deposit these things without injury; and there were conveniences for washing. They were healthy in appearance, many of them remarkably so, and had the manners and deportment of young women: not of degraded brutes of burden. If I had seen in one of those mills (but I did not, though I looked for something of this kind with a sharp eye), the most lisping, mincing, affected, and ridiculous young creature that my imagination could suggest, I should have thought of the careless, moping, slatternly, degraded, dull reverse (I HAVE seen that), and should have been still well pleased to look upon her.

The rooms in which they worked, were as well ordered as themselves. In the windows of some, there were green plants, which were trained to shade the glass; in all, there was as much fresh air, cleanliness, and comfort, as the nature of the occupation would possibly admit of. Out of so large a number of females, many of whom were only then just verging upon womanhood, it may be reasonably supposed that some were delicate and fragile in appearance: no doubt there were. But I solemnly declare, that from all the crowd I saw in the different factories that day, I cannot recall or separate one young face that gave me a painful impression; not one young girl whom, assuming it to be a matter of necessity that she should gain her daily bread by the labour of her hands, I would have removed from those works if I had had the power.

They reside in various boarding-houses near at hand. The owners of the mills are particularly careful to allow no persons to enter upon the possession of these houses, whose characters have not undergone the most searching and thorough inquiry. Any complaint that is made against them, by the boarders, or by any one else, is fully investigated; and if good ground of complaint be shown to exist against them, they are removed, and their occupation is handed over to some more deserving person. There are a few children employed in these factories, but not many. The laws of the State forbid their working more than nine months in the year, and require that they be educated during the other three. For this purpose there are schools in Lowell; and there are churches and chapels of various persuasions, in which the young women may observe that form of worship in which they have been educated.

At some distance from the factories, and on the highest and pleasantest ground in the neighbourhood, stands their hospital, or boarding-house for the sick: it is the best house in those parts, and was built by an eminent merchant for his own residence. Like that institution at Boston, which I have before described, it is not parcelled out into wards, but is divided into convenient chambers, each of which has all the comforts of a very comfortable home.

The principal medical attendant resides under the same roof; and were the patients members of his own family, they could not be better cared for, or attended with greater gentleness and consideration. The weekly charge in this establishment for each female patient is three dollars, or twelve shillings English; but no girl employed by any of the corporations is ever excluded for want of the means of payment. That they do not very often want the means, may be gathered from the fact, that in July, 1841, no fewer than nine hundred and seventy-eight of these girls were depositors in the Lowell Savings Bank: the amount of whose joint savings was estimated at one hundred thousand dollars, or twenty thousand English pounds.

I am now going to state three facts, which will startle a large class of readers on this side of the Atlantic, very much.

Firstly, there is a joint-stock piano in a great many of the boarding-houses. Secondly, nearly all these young ladies subscribe to circulating libraries. Thirdly, they have got up among themselves a periodical called THE LOWELL OFFERING, 'A repository of original articles, written exclusively by females actively employed in the mills,' – which is duly printed, published, and sold; and whereof I brought away from Lowell four hundred good solid pages, which I have read from beginning to end.

The large class of readers, startled by these facts, will exclaim, with one voice, 'How very preposterous!' On my deferentially inquiring why, they will answer, 'These things are above their station.' In reply to that objection, I would beg to ask what their station is.

It is their station to work. And they DO work. They labour in these mills, upon an average, twelve hours a day, which is unques-tionably work, and pretty tight work too. Perhaps it is above their station to indulge in such amusements, on any terms. Are we quite sure that we in England have not formed our ideas of the 'station' of working people, from accustoming ourselves to the contemplation of that class as they are, and not as they might be? I think that if we examine our own feelings, we shall find that the pianos, and the circulating libraries, and even the Lowell Offering, startle us by their novelty, and not by their bearing upon any abstract question of right or wrong.

For myself, I know no station in which, the occupation of to-day cheerfully done and the occupation of to-morrow cheerfully looked to, any one of these pursuits is not most humanising and laudable. I know no station which is rendered more endurable to the person in it, or more safe to the person out of it, by having ignorance for its associate. I know no station which has a right to monopolise the means of mutual instruction, improvement, and rational entertainment; or which has ever continued to be a station very long, after seeking to do so.

Of the merits of the Lowell Offering as a literary production, I will only observe, putting entirely out of sight the fact of the articles having been written by these girls after the arduous labours of the day, that it will compare advantageously with a great many English Annuals. It is pleasant to find that many of its Tales are of the Mills and of those who work in them; that they inculcate habits of self-denial and contentment, and teach good doctrines of enlarged benevolence.

A strong feeling for the beauties of nature, as displayed in the solitudes the writers have left at home, breathes through its pages like wholesome village air; and though a circulating library is a favourable school for the study of such topics, it has very scant allusion to fine clothes, fine marriages, fine houses, or fine life. Some persons might object to the papers being signed occasionally with rather fine names, but this is an American fashion. One of the provinces of the state legislature of Massachusetts is to alter ugly names into pretty ones, as the children improve upon the tastes of their parents. These changes costing little or nothing, scores of Mary Annes are solemnly converted into Bevelinas every session.

It is said that on the occasion of a visit from General Jackson or General Harrison to this town (I forget which, but it is not to the purpose), he walked through three miles and a half of these young ladies all dressed out with parasols and silk stockings. But as I am not aware that any worse consequence ensued, than a sudden looking-up of all the parasols and silk stockings in the market; and perhaps the bankruptcy of some speculative New Englander who bought them all up at any price, in expectation of a demand that never came; I set no great store by the circumstance.

In this brief account of Lowell, and inadequate expression of the gratification it yielded me, and cannot fail to afford to any foreigner to whom the condition of such people at home is a subject of interest and anxious speculation, I have carefully abstained from drawing a comparison between these factories and those of our own land. Many of the circumstances whose strong influence has been at work for years in our manufacturing towns have not arisen here; and there is no manufacturing population in Lowell, so to speak: for these girls (often the daughters of small farmers) come from other States, remain a few years in the mills, and then go home for good.

The contrast would be a strong one, for it would be between the Good and Evil, the living light and deepest shadow. I abstain from it, because I deem it just to do so. But I only the more earnestly adjure all those whose eyes may rest on these pages, to pause and reflect upon the difference between this town and those great haunts of desperate misery: to call to mind, if they can in the midst of party strife and squabble, the efforts that must be made to purge them of their suffering and danger: and last, and foremost, to remember how the precious Time is rushing by.

I returned at night by the same railroad and in the same kind of car. One of the passengers being exceedingly anxious to expound at great length to my companion (not to me, of course) the true principles on which books of travel in America should be written by Englishmen, I feigned to fall asleep. But glancing all the way out at window from the corners of my eyes, I found abundance of entertainment for the rest of the ride in watching the effects of the wood fire, which had been invisible in the morning but were now brought out in full relief by the darkness: for we were travelling in a whirlwind of bright sparks, which showered about us like a storm of fiery snow.

The second extract is from Chapter 21 of *Martin Chuzzlewit*. Martin Chuzzlewit and Mark Tapley arrive in America in Chapter 16 of the novel and stay initially in New York. In Chapter 21 they embark on the railway journey described here to the fictitious town of Watertoast, where they are deceived by characters offering opportunities to invest their limited finances in land and property in Eden, which turns out to be little more than a disease-ridden swamp.

The Railroad to Watertoast

How the wheels clank and rattle, and the tram-road shakes, as the train rushes on! And now the engine yells, as it were lashed and tortured like a living labourer, and writhed in agony. A poor fancy; for steel and iron are of infinitely greater account, in this commonwealth, than flesh and blood. If the cunning work of man be urged beyond its power of endurance, it has within it the elements of its own revenge; whereas the wretched mechanism of the Divine Hand is dangerous with no such property, but may be tampered with, and crushed, and broken, at the driver's pleasure. Look at that engine! It shall cost a man more dollars in the way of penalty and fine, and satisfaction of the outraged law, to deface in wantonness that senseless mass of metal, than to take the lives of twenty human creatures! Thus the stars wink upon the bloody stripes; and Liberty pulls down her cap upon her eyes, and owns oppression in its vilest aspect, for her sister.

The engine-driver of the train whose noise awoke us to the present chapter was certainly troubled with no such reflections as these; nor is it very probable that his mind was disturbed by any reflections at all. He leaned with folded arms and crossed legs against the side of the carriage, smoking: and, except when he expressed, by a grunt as short as his pipe, his approval of some particularly dexterous aim on the part of his colleague, the fireman, who beguiled his leisure by throwing logs of wood from the tender at the numerous stray cattle on the line, he preserved a composure so immovable, and an indifference so complete, that if the locomotive had been a sucking-pig, he could not have been more perfectly indifferent to its doings. Notwithstanding the tranquil state of this officer, and his unbroken peace of mind, the train was proceeding with tolerable rapidity; and the rails being but poorly laid, the jolts and bumps it met with in its progress were neither slight nor few.

There were three great caravans or cars attached. The ladies' car, the gentlemen's car, and the car for negroes: the latter painted black, as an appropriate compliment to its company. Martin and Mark Tapley were in the first, as it was the most comfortable; and, being far from full, received other gentlemen who, like them, were unblessed by the society of ladies of their own. They were seated side by side, and were engaged in earnest conversation.

'And so, Mark', said Martin, looking at him with an anxious expression, 'and so you are glad we have left New York far behind us, are you?'

'Yes, sir', said Mark. 'I am. Precious glad.'

'Were you not "jolly" there?' asked Martin.

'On the contrary, sir', returned Mark. 'The jolliest week as ever I spent in my life, was that there week at Pawkins's.'

'What do you think of our prospects?' inquired Martin, with an air that plainly said he had avoided the question for some time.

'Uncommon bright, sir', returned Mark. 'Impossible for a place to have a better name, sir, than the Walley of Eden. No man couldn't think of settling in a better place than the Walley of Eden. And I'm told,' added Mark, after a pause, 'as there's lots of serpents there, so we shall come out quite complete and reg'lar.'

So far from dwelling upon this agreeable piece of information with the least dismay, Mark's face grew radiant as he called it to mind: so very radiant, that a stranger might have supposed he had all his life been yearning for the society of serpents, and now hailed with delight the approaching consummation of his fondest wishes.

7

TRAVELS IN AND
TO FRANCE

Première année — N° 21   Un numéro : **10** centimes   14 Juin 1868

L'ECLIPSE

CHARLES DICKENS — par GILL

Travelling to France, either to stay there or move on to other parts of Europe like Italy and Switzerland, figures significantly in Dickens's journeying. He was very fond of France, and fluent in spoken and written forms of the language, referring to himself as *'Français naturalise, et Citoyen de Paris'* (naturalised Frenchman and citizen of Paris).

Dickens made his first visit to France in 1837 and his last in 1868. His European travelling spans 31 years, and includes some long periods of residence abroad during the 1840s, and some frequent shorter visits to the northern coast of France later in his life. He enjoyed visits to Boulogne-sur-mer, which he called 'Our French Watering Place', took his family on holiday there in 1853, 1854 and 1856, and formed close friendships with local people. Later, in 1862, 1863 and 1865, he visited nearby Condette, accompanied by Ellen Ternan. In January 1863 he did a spectacularly successful series of public readings at the British Embassy in Paris. He enjoyed the freedom of a different but nearby country and culture, and took advantage of the new transport developments to permit increasing ease and frequency of visits, especially now that Europe was opening up after the defeat of Napoleon in 1815. There were, however, risks, as will be seen in Chapter 10.

Dickens made his first trip to Paris by the South Eastern Railway's new 'Double Special Express Service' in 1850, travelling overnight from London Bridge Station on 22/23 June, arriving in Paris at 8.45 a.m. 'The twelve hours' journey here is astounding,' he wrote to John Forster, his biographer, ' – marvellously done, except in the means of refreshment, which are absolutely none.' 'A Flight', published in *Household Words* on 30 August 1851, gives a wonderful description of a high-speed journey, from London to Paris, again identifying the unsettling quality of travel, such a new experience for the time.

However, the South Eastern Railway Company's advertisement in *Bradshaw* in August 1851 shows the company was already keen to reduce the time it took:

> London to Paris in 11 hours by Special express Train and Steam Ship in correspondence via Folkestone and Boulogne and Dover and Calais alternately, changing the time of departure to suite the tide and prevent all delay. There are also special trains and steamers between London and Paris by the same route each evening.

One cannot help but feel Dickens would have been both astonished and intrigued at the thought that his journey might one day be done in just over two hours! 'A Flight' indeed. On arriving in Paris, he adjusts to the new city in the essay's concluding paragraph.

A Flight

When Don Diego de —— I forget his name – the inventor of the last new Flying Machines, price so many francs for ladies, so many more for gentlemen – when Don Diego, by permission of Deputy Chaff Wax and his noble band, shall have taken out a Patent for the Queen's dominions, and shall have opened a commodious Warehouse in an airy situation; and when all persons of any gentility will keep at least a pair of wings, and be seen skimming about in every direction; I shall take a flight to Paris (as I soar round the world) in a cheap and independent manner. At present, my reliance is on the South-Eastern Railway Company, in whose Express Train here I sit, at eight of the clock on a very hot morning, under the very hot roof of the Terminus at London Bridge, in danger of being 'forced' like a cucumber or a melon, or a pine-apple. And talking of pine-apples, I suppose there never were so many pine-apples in a Train as there appear to be in this Train.

Whew! The hot-house air is faint with pine-apples. Every French citizen or citizeness is carrying pine-apples home. The compact little Enchantress in the corner of my carriage (French actress, to whom I yielded up my heart under the auspices of that brave child, 'MEAT-CHELL,' at the Saint James's Theatre the night before last) has a pine-apple in her lap. Compact Enchantress's friend, confidante, mother, mystery, Heaven knows what, has two pine-apples in her lap, and a bundle of them under the seat. Tobacco-smoky Frenchman in Algerine wrapper, with peaked hood behind, who might be Abd-el-Kader dyed rifle-green, and who seems to be dressed entirely in dirt and braid, carries pine-apples in a covered basket. Tall, grave, melancholy Frenchman, with black Vandyke beard, arid hair close-cropped, with expansive chest to waistcoat, and compressive waist to coat: saturnine as to his pantaloons, calm as to his feminine boots, precious as to his jewellery, smooth and white as to his linen: dark-eyed, high-foreheaded, hawk-nosed – got up, one thinks, like Lucifer or Mephistopheles, or Zamiel, transformed into a highly genteel Parisian – has the green end of a pine-apple sticking out of his neat valise.

Whew! If I were to be kept here long, under this forcing-frame, I wonder what would become of me – whether I should be forced into a giant, or should sprout or blow into some other phenomenon! Compact Enchantress is not rued by the heat – she is always composed, always compact. O look at her little ribbons, frills, and edges, at her shawl, at her gloves, at her hair, at her bracelets, at her bonnet, at everything about her! How is it accomplished? What does she do to be so neat? How is it that every trifle she wears belongs to her, and cannot choose but be a part of her? And even Mystery, look at *her*! A model. Mystery is not young, not pretty, though still of an average candlelight passability; but she does such miracles in her own behalf, that, one of these days, when she dies, they'll be amazed to find an old woman in her bed, distantly like her. She was an actress once, I shouldn't wonder, and had a Mystery attendant on herself. Perhaps, Compact Enchantress will live to be a Mystery, and to wait with a shawl at the side scenes, and to sit opposite to Mademoiselle in railway carriages, and smile and talk subserviently, as Mystery does now. That's hard to believe!

Two Englishmen, and now our carriage is full. First Englishman, in the monied interest – flushed, highly respectable – Stock Exchange, perhaps – City, certainly. Faculties of second Englishman entirely absorbed in hurry. Plunges into the carriage, blind. Calls out of window concerning his luggage, deaf. Suffocates himself under pillows of great coats, for no reason, and in a demented manner. Will receive no assurance from any porter whatsoever. Is stout and hot, and wipes his head, and makes himself hotter by breathing so hard. Is totally incredulous respecting assurance of Collected Guard that 'there's no hurry.' No hurry! And a Flight to Paris in eleven hours!

It is all one to me in this drowsy corner, hurry, or no hurry. Until Don Diego shall send home my wings, my flight is with the South-Eastern Company. I can fly with the South-Eastern, more lazily, at all events, than in the upper air. I have but to sit here thinking as idly as I please, and be whisked away. I am not accountable to anybody for the idleness of my thoughts in such an idle summer flight; my flight is provided for by the South-Eastern, and is no business of mine.

The bell! With all my heart. It does not require *me* to do so much as even to flap my wings. Something snorts for me, something shrieks for me, something proclaims to everything else that it had better keep out of my way, – and away I go. Ah! The fresh air is pleasant after the forcing-frame, though it does blow over these interminable streets, and scatter the smoke of this vast wilderness of chimneys. Here we are – no, I mean there we were, for it has darted far into the rear – in Bermondsey where the tanners live. Flash! The distant shipping in the Thames is gone. Whirr! The little streets of new brick and red tile, with here and there a flagstaff growing like a tall weed out of the scarlet beans, and, everywhere, plenty of open sewer and ditch for the promotion of the public health, have been fired off in a volley. Whizz! Dustheaps, market-gardens, and waste grounds. Rattle! New Cross Station. Shock! There we were at Croydon. Bur-r-r-r! The tunnel.

I wonder why it is that when I shut my eyes in a tunnel I begin to feel as if I were going at an Express pace the other way. I am clearly going back to London now. Compact Enchantress must have forgotten something, and reversed the engine. No! After long darkness, pale fitful streaks of light appear. I am still flying on for Folkestone. The streaks grow stronger become continuous – become the ghost of day – become the living day – became I mean – the tunnel is miles and miles away, and here I fly through sunlight, all among the harvest and the Kentish hops.

There is a dreamy pleasure in this flying. I wonder where it was, and when it was, that we exploded, blew into space somehow, a Parliamentary Train, with a crowd of heads and faces looking at us out of cages, and some hats waving. Monied Interest says it was at Reigate Station. Expounds to Mystery how Reigate Station is so many miles from London, which Mystery again develops to Compact Enchantress. There might be neither a Reigate nor a London for me, as I fly away among the Kentish hops and harvest. What do *I* care!

Bang! We have let another Station off, and fly away regardless. Everything is flying. The hop-gardens turn gracefully towards me, presenting regular avenues of hops in rapid flight, then whirl away. So do the pools and rushes, haystacks, sheep, clover in full bloom delicious to the sight and smell, corn-sheaves, cherry-orchards, apple-orchards, reapers, gleaners, hedges, gates, fields that taper off into little angular corners, cottages, gardens, now and then a church. Bang, bang! A double-barrelled Station! Now a wood, now a bridge, now a landscape, now a cutting, now a – Bang! a single-barrelled Station – there was a cricket match somewhere with two white tents, and then four flying cows, then turnips – now, the wires of the electric telegraph are all alive, and spin, and blurr their edges, and go up and down, and make the intervals between each other most irregular: contracting and expanding in the strangest manner. Now we slacken. With a screwing, and a grinding, and a smell of water thrown on ashes, now we stop!

Demented Traveller, who has been for two or three minutes watchful, clutches his great-coats, plunges at the door, rattles it, cries 'Hi!' eager to embark on board of impossible packets, far inland. Collected Guard appears. 'Are you for Tunbridge, Sir?'

'Tunbridge? No. Paris.'

'Plenty of time, Sir. No hurry. Five minutes here, Sir, for refresh-ment.' I am so blest (anticipating Zamiel, by half a second) as to procure a glass of water for Compact Enchantress.

Who would suppose we had been flying at such a rate, and shall take wing again directly? Refreshment-room full, platform full, porter with watering-pot deliberately cooling a hot wheel, other porter with equal deliberation helping the rest of the wheels boun-tifully to ice cream. Monied Interest and I re-entering the carriage first, and being there alone, he intimates to me that the French are 'no go' as a Nation.

I ask why?

He says, that Reign of Terror of theirs was quite enough.

I ventured to inquire whether he remembers anything that preceded said Reign of Terror?

He says, not particularly.

'Because', I remark, 'the harvest that is reaped, has sometimes been sown.'

Monied Interest repeats, as quite enough for him, that the French are revolutionary, – 'and always at it'.

Bell. Compact Enchantress, helped in by Zamiel, (whom the stars confound!) gives us her charming little side-box look, and smites me to the core. Mystery eating sponge-cake. Pine-apple atmosphere faintly tinged with suspicions of sherry. Demented Traveller flits past the carriage, looking for it. Is blind with agitation, and can't see it. Seems singled out by Destiny to be the only unhappy creature in the flight, who has any cause to hurry himself. Is nearly left behind. Is seized by Collected Guard after the Train is in motion, and bundled in. Still, has lingering suspicions that there must be a boat in the neighbourhood, and *will* look wildly out of window for it.

Flight resumed. Corn-sheaves, hop-gardens, reapers, glean-ers, apple- orchards, cherry orchards, Stations single and double-barrelled, Ashford. Compact Enchantress (constantly talking to Mystery, in an exquisite manner) gives a little scream; a sound that seems to come from high up in her precious little head; from behind her bright little eyebrows. 'Great Heaven, my pine-apple! My Angel! It is lost!' Mystery is desolated. A search made. It is not lost. Zamiel finds it. I curse him (flying) in the Persian manner. May his face be turned upside down, and jackasses sit upon his uncle's grave!

Now fresher air, now glimpses of unenclosed Down-land with flapping crows flying over it whom we soon outfly, now the Sea, now Folkestone at a quarter after ten. 'Tickets ready, gentlemen!' Demented dashes at the door. 'For Paris, Sir? No hurry.'

Not the least. We are dropped slowly down to the Port, and sidle to and fro (the whole Train) before the insensible Royal George Hotel, for some ten minutes. The Royal George takes no more heed of us than its namesake under water at Spithead, or under earth at Windsor, does. The Royal George's dog lies winking and blinking at us, without taking the trouble to sit up; and the Royal George's 'wedding party' at the open window (who seem, I must say, rather tired of bliss) don't bestow a solitary glance upon us, flying thus to Paris in eleven hours. The first gentleman in Folkestone is evidently used up, on this subject.

Meanwhile, Demented chafes. Conceives that every man's hand is against him, and exerting itself to prevent his getting to Paris. Refuses consolation. Rattles door. Sees smoke on the horizon, and 'knows' it's the boat gone without him. Monied Interest resentfully explains that he is going to Paris too. Demented signifies that if Monied Interest chooses to be left behind, *he* don't.

'Refreshments in the Waiting-Room, ladies and gentlemen. No hurry, ladies and gentlemen, for Paris. No hurry whatever!'

Twenty minutes' pause, by Folkestone clock, for looking at Enchantress while she eats a sandwich, and at Mystery while she eats of everything there that is eatable, from pork-pie, sausage, jam, and gooseberries, to lumps of sugar. All this time, there is a very waterfall of luggage, with a spray of dust, tumbling slant-wise from the pier into the steamboat. All this time, Demented (who has no business with it) watches it with starting eyes, fiercely requiring to be shown *his* luggage. When it at last concludes the cataract, he rushes hotly to refresh – is shouted after, pursued, jostled, brought back, pitched into the departing steamer upside down, and caught by mariners disgracefully.

A lovely harvest-day, a cloudless sky, a tranquil sea. The piston-rods of the engines so regularly coming up from below, to look (as well they may) at the bright weather, and so regularly almost knocking their iron heads against the cross beam of the skylight, and never doing it! Another Parisian actress is on board, attended by another Mystery. Compact Enchantress greets her sister artist – Oh, the Compact One's pretty teeth! – and Mystery greets Mystery. *My* Mystery soon ceases to be conversational – is taken poorly, in a word, having lunched too miscellaneously – and goes below. The remaining Mystery then smiles upon the sister artists (who, I am afraid, wouldn't greatly mind stabbing each other), and is upon the whole ravished.

And now I find that all the French people on board begin to grow, and all the English people to shrink. The French are nearing home, and shaking off a disadvantage, whereas we are shaking it on. Zamiel is the same man, and Abd-el-Kader is the same man, but each seems to come into possession of an indescribable confidence that departs from us – from Monied Interest, for instance, and from me. Just what they gain, we lose. Certain British 'Gents' about the steersman, intellectually nurtured at home on parody of everything and truth of nothing, become subdued, and in a manner forlorn; and when the steersman tells them (not unexultingly) how he has 'been upon this station now eight year, and never see the old town of Bullun yet,' one of them, with an imbecile reliance on a reed, asks him what he considers to be the best hotel in Paris?

Now, I tread upon French ground, and am greeted by the three charming words, Liberty, Equality, Fraternity, painted up (in letters a little too thin for their height) on the Custom House wall – also by the sight of large cocked hats, without which demonstrative head-gear nothing of a public nature can be done upon this soil. All the rabid Hotel population of Boulogne howl and shriek outside a distant barrier, frantic to get at us. Demented, by some unlucky means peculiar to himself, is delivered over to their fury, and is presently seen struggling in a whirlpool of Touters – is somehow understood to be going to Paris – is, with infinite noise, rescued by two cocked hats, and brought into Custom House bondage with the rest of us.

Here, I resign the active duties of life to an eager being, of preternatural sharpness, with a shelving forehead and a shabby snuff-coloured coat, who (from the wharf) brought me down with his eye before the boat came into port. He darts upon my luggage, on the floor where all the luggage is strewn like a wreck at the bottom of the great deep; gets it proclaimed and weighed as the property of 'Monsieur a traveller unknown'; pays certain francs for it, to a certain functionary behind a Pigeon Hole, like a paybox at a Theatre (the arrangements in general are on a wholesale scale, half military and half theatrical); and I suppose I shall find it when I come to Paris – he says I shall. I know nothing about it, except that I pay him his small fee, and pocket the ticket he gives me, and sit upon a counter, involved in the general distraction.

Railway station. 'Lunch or dinner, ladies and gentlemen. Plenty of time for Paris. Plenty of time!' Large hall, long counter, long strips of dining-table, bottles of wine, plates of meat, roast chickens, little loaves of bread, basins of soup, little caraffes of brandy, cakes, and fruit. Comfortably restored from these resources, I begin to fly again.

I saw Zamiel (before I took wing) presented to Compact Enchantress and Sister Artist, by an officer in uniform, with a waist like a wasp's, and pantaloons like two balloons. They all got into the next carriage together, accompanied by the two Mysteries. They laughed. I am alone in the carriage (for I don't consider Demented anybody) and alone in the world.

Fields, windmills, low grounds, pollard-trees, windmills, fields, fortifications, Abbeville, soldiering and drumming. I wonder where England is, and when I was there last – about two years ago, I should say. Flying in and out among these trenches and batteries, skimming the clattering drawbridges, looking down into the stagnant ditches, I become a prisoner of state, escaping. I am confined with a comrade in a fortress. Our room is in an upper story. We have tried to get up the chimney, but there's an iron grating across it, imbedded in the masonry. After months of labour, we have worked the grating loose with the poker, and can lift it up. We have also made a hook, and twisted our rugs and blankets into ropes. Our plan is, to go up the chimney, hook our ropes to the top, descend hand over hand upon the roof of the guard-house far below, shake the hook loose, watch the opportunity of the sentinel's pacing away, hook again, drop into the ditch, swim across it, creep into the shelter of the wood. The time is come a wild and stormy night. We are up the chimney, we are on the guard-house roof, we are swimming in the murky ditch, when, lo! *'Qui v'là?'* a bugle, the alarm, a crash! What is it? Death? No, Amiens.

More fortifications, more soldiering and drumming, more basins of soup, more little loaves of bread, more bottles of wine, more caraffes of brandy, more time for refreshment. Everything good, and everything ready. Bright, unsubstantial-looking, scenic sort of station. People waiting. Houses, uniforms, beards, moustaches, some sabots, plenty of neat women, and a few old-visaged children. Unless it be a delusion born of my giddy flight, the grown-up people and the children seem to change places in France. In general, the boys and girls are little old men and women, and the men and women lively boys and girls.

Bugle, shriek, flight resumed. Monied Interest has come into my carriage. Says the manner of refreshing is 'not bad', but considers it French. Admits great dexterity and politeness in the attendants. Thinks a decimal currency may have something to do with their despatch in settling accounts, and don't know but what it's sensible and convenient. Adds, however, as a general protest, that they're a revolutionary people and always at it.

Ramparts, canals, cathedral, river, soldiering and drumming, open country, river, earthenware manufactures, Creil. Again ten minutes. Not even Demented in a hurry. Station, a drawing-room with a verandah: like a planter's house. Monied Interest considers it a bandbox, and not made to last. Little round tables in it, at one of which the Sister Artists and attendant Mysteries are established with Wasp and Zamiel, as if they were going to stay a week.

Anon, with no more trouble than before, I am flying again, and lazily wondering as I fly. What has the South-Eastern done with all the horrible little villages we used to pass through, in the *Diligence*? What have they done with all the summer dust, with all the winter mud, with all the dreary avenues of little trees, with all the ramshackle postyards, with all the beggars (who used to turn out at night with bits of lighted candle, to look in at the coach windows), with all the long-tailed horses who were always biting one another, with all the big postillions in jack-boots — with all the mouldy cafés that we used to stop at, where a long mildewed tablecloth, set forth with jovial bottles of vinegar and oil, and with a Siamese arrangement of pepper and salt, was never wanting? Where are the grass-grown little towns, the wonderful little market-places all unconscious of markets, the shops that nobody kept, the streets that nobody trod, the churches that nobody went to, the bells that nobody rang, the tumble-down old buildings plastered with many-coloured bills that nobody read? Where are the two-and-twenty weary hours of long long day and night journey, sure to be either insupportably hot or insupportably cold? Where are the pains in my bones, where are the fidgets in my legs, where is the Frenchman with the nightcap who never *would* have the little coupé- window down, and who always fell upon me when he went to sleep, and always slept all night snoring onions?

A voice breaks in with 'Paris! Here we are!'

I have overflown myself, perhaps, but I can't believe it. I feel as if I were enchanted or bewitched. It is barely eight o'clock yet – it is nothing like half-past – when I have had my luggage examined at that briskest of Custom-Houses attached to the station, and am rattling over the pavement in a Hackney cabriolet.

Surely, not the pavement of Paris? Yes, I think it is, too. I don't know any other place where there are all these high houses, all these haggard-looking wine shops, all these billiard tables, all these stocking-makers with flat red or yellow legs of wood for sign-board, all these fuel shops with stacks of billets painted outside, and real billets sawing in the gutter, all these dirty corners of streets, all these cabinet pictures over dark doorways representing discreet matrons nursing babies. And yet this morning – I'll think of it in a warm-bath.

Very like a small room that I remember in the Chinese baths upon the Boulevard, certainly; and, though I see it through the steam, I think that I might swear to that peculiar hot-linen- basket, like a large wicker hour-glass. When can it have been that I left home? When was it that I paid 'through to Paris' at London Bridge, and discharged myself of all responsibility, except the preservation of a voucher ruled into three divisions, of which the first was snipped off at Folkestone, the second aboard the boat, and the third taken at my journey's end? It seems to have been ages ago. Calculation is useless. I will go out for a walk.

The crowds in the streets, the lights in the shops and balconies, the elegance, variety, and beauty of their decorations, the number of the theatres, the brilliant cafés with their windows thrown up high and their vivacious groups at little tables on the pavement, the light and glitter of the houses turned as it were inside out, soon convince me that it is no dream; that I am in Paris, howsoever I got here. I stroll down to the sparkling Palais Royal, up the Rue de Rivoli, to the Place Vendôme. As I glance into a print-shop window, Monied

Interest, my late travelling companion, comes upon me, laughing with the highest relish of disdain. 'Here's a people!' he says, pointing to Napoleon in the window and Napoleon on the column. 'Only one idea all over Paris! A monomania!' Humph! I THINK I have seen Napoleon's match? There WAS a statue, when I came away, at Hyde Park Corner, and another in the City, and a print or two in the shops.

I walk up to the Barrière de l'Etoile, sufficiently dazed by my flight to have a pleasant doubt of the reality of everything about me; of the lively crowd, the overhanging trees, the performing dogs, the hobby-horses, the beautiful perspectives of shining lamps: the hundred and one enclosures, where the singing is, in gleaming orchestras of azure and gold, and where a star-eyed Houri comes round with a box for voluntary offerings. So, I pass to my hotel, enchanted; sup, enchanted; go to bed, enchanted; pushing back this morning (if it really were this morning) into the remoteness of time, blessing the South-Eastern Company for realising the Arabian Nights in these prose days, murmuring, as I wing my idle flight into the laud of dreams, 'No hurry, ladies and gentlemen, going to Paris in eleven hours. It is so well done, that there really is no hurry!'

The second extract in this chapter is taken from an essay published in *All the Year Round* on 2 May 1863. It describes the experience of travelling across the English Channel on a packet-boat and the reception travellers encounter once arrived in France. It is, like some others published from 1860, one of the 'Uncommercial Traveller' essays. The extract begins on arrival in Calais.

From 'The Calais Night Mail'

C alais up and doing at the railway station, and Calais down and dreaming in its bed; Calais with something of 'an ancient and fish-like smell' about it, and Calais blown and sea-washed pure; Calais represented at the Buffet by savoury roast fowls, hot coffee, cognac, and Bordeaux; and Calais represented everywhere by flitting persons with a monomania for changing money – though I never shall be able to understand in my present state of existence how they live by it, but I suppose I should, if I understood the currency question – Calais *en gros*, and Calais *en detail*, forgive one who has deeply wronged you. – I was not fully aware of it on the other side, but I meant Dover.

Ding, ding! To the carriages, gentlemen the travellers. Ascend, then, gentlemen the travellers, for Hazebroucke, Lille, Douai, Bruxelles, Arras, Amiens, and Paris! I, humble representative of the uncommercial interest, ascend with the rest. The train is light to-night, and I share my compartment with but two fellow- travellers; one, a compatriot in an obsolete cravat, who thinks it a quite unaccountable thing that they don't keep 'London time' on a French railway, and who is made angry by my modestly suggesting the possibility of Paris time being more in their way; the other, a young priest, with a very small bird in a very small cage, who feeds the small bird with a quill, and then puts him up in the network above his head, where he advances twittering, to his front wires, and seems to address me in an electioneering manner. The compatriot (who crossed in the boat, and whom I judge to be some person of distinction, as he was shut up, like a stately species of rabbit, in a private hutch on deck) and the young priest (who joined us at Calais) are soon asleep, and then the bird and I have it all to ourselves.

A stormy night still; a night that sweeps the wires of the electric telegraph with a wild and fitful hand; a night so very stormy, with the added storm of the train-progress through it, that when the Guard comes clambering round to mark the tickets while we are at full speed (a really horrible performance in an express train, though he holds on to the open window by his elbows in the most deliberate manner), he stands in such a whirlwind that I grip him fast by the collar, and feel it next to manslaughter to let him go. Still, when he is gone, the small, small bird remains at his front wires feebly twittering to me – twittering and twittering, until, leaning back in my place and looking at him in drowsy fascination, I find that he seems to jog my memory as we rush along.

Uncommercial travels (thus the small, small bird) have lain in their idle thriftless way through all this range of swamp and dyke, as through many other odd places; and about here, as you very well know, are the queer old stone farm-houses, approached by drawbridges, and the windmills that you get at by boats. Here, are the lands where the women hoe and dig, paddling canoe-wise from field to field, and here are the cabarets and other peasant-houses where the stone dove-cotes in the littered yards are as strong as warders' towers in old castles. Here, are the long monotonous miles of canal, with the great Dutch-built barges garishly painted, and the towing girls, sometimes harnessed by the forehead, sometimes by the girdle and the shoulders, not a pleasant sight to see. Scattered through this country are mighty works of VAUBAN, whom you know about, and regiments of such corporals as you heard of once upon a time, and many a blue-eyed Bebelle. Through these flat districts, in the shining summer days, walk those long, grotesque files of young novices in enormous shovel-hats, whom you remember blackening the ground checkered by the avenues of leafy trees. And now that Hazebroucke slumbers certain kilometres ahead, recall the summer evening when your dusty feet strolling up from the station tended hap-hazard to a Fair there, where the oldest inhabitants were circling round and round a barrel-organ on hobby- horses, with the greatest gravity, and where the principal show in the Fair was a Religious Richardson's – literally, on its own announcement in great letters, THEATRE RELIGIEUX. In which improving Temple, the dramatic representation was of 'all the interesting events in the life of our Lord, from the Manger to the Tomb'; the principal female character, without any reservation or exception, being at the moment of your arrival, engaged in trimming the external Moderators (as it was growing dusk), while the next principal female character took the money, and the Young Saint John disported himself upside down on the platform.

Looking up at this point to confirm the small, small bird in every particular he has mentioned, I find he has ceased to twitter, and has put his head under his wing. Therefore, in my different way I follow the good example.

8

DANGER AND DISASTER:
IN THE IMAGINATION

From the very beginning, death on the railway was all too visible. William Huskisson MP was killed at the opening of the Liverpool to Manchester railway on 15 September 1830. This final selection from *Dombey and Son* focuses on Chapter 55, as the plot leads remorselessly forward to the death on the railway of the novel's villain, James Carker.

Carker is the Manager of Mr Dombey's business interests, but he is engaged in a process of undermining and exploiting him, both professionally and personally. By the time we reach this chapter, Carker has tempted Dombey's second wife, Edith, to leave her husband and travel to Dijon in France, where he will meet her. Dombey discovers the plan and pursues Carker when he goes to France. Once Carker and Edith meet, she rejects him implacably and he embarks on a return journey to England in order to avoid his pursuer. Once returned, he sees Dombey following him and falls in front of an oncoming train. It is the first example of a novel's villain being destroyed by a train. The chapter is given in full to illustrate Dickens's skill in developing a narrative towards a climax.

The Death of Carker

The Porter at the iron gate which shut the court-yard from the street, had left the little wicket of his house open, and was gone away; no doubt to mingle in the distant noise at the door of the great staircase. Lifting the latch softly, Carker crept out, and shutting the jangling gate after him with as little noise as possible, hurried off.

In the fever of his mortification and unavailing rage, the panic that had seized upon him mastered him completely. It rose to such a height that he would have blindly encountered almost any risk, rather than meet the man of whom, two hours ago, he had been utterly regardless. His fierce arrival, which he had never expected; the sound of his voice; their having been so near a meeting, face to face; he would have braved out this, after the first momentary shock of alarm, and would have put as bold a front upon his guilt as any villain. But the springing of his mine upon himself, seemed to have rent and shivered all his hardihood and self-reliance. Spurned like any reptile; entrapped and mocked; turned upon, and trodden down by the proud woman whose mind he had slowly poisoned, as he thought, until she had sunk into the mere creature of his pleasure; undeceived in his deceit, and with his fox's hide stripped off, he sneaked away, abashed, degraded, and afraid.

Some other terror came upon him quite removed from this of being pursued, suddenly, like an electric shock, as he was creeping through the streets Some visionary terror, unintelligible and inexplicable, associated with a trembling of the ground, – a rush and sweep of something through the air, like Death upon the wing. He shrunk, as if to let the thing go by. It was not gone, it never had been there, yet what a startling horror it had left behind.

He raised his wicked face so full of trouble, to the night sky, where the stars, so full of peace, were shining on him as they had been when he first stole out into the air; and stopped to think what he should do. The dread of being hunted in a strange remote place, where the laws might not protect him – the novelty of the feeling that it was strange and remote, originating in his being left alone so suddenly amid the ruins of his plans – his greater dread of seeking refuge now, in Italy or in Sicily, where men might be hired to assassinate him, he thought, at any dark street corner – the waywardness of guilt and fear – perhaps some sympathy of action with the turning back of all his schemes – impelled him to turn back too, and go to England.

'I am safer there, in any case. If I should not decide,' he thought, 'to give this fool a meeting, I am less likely to be traced there, than abroad here, now. And if I should (this cursed fit being over), at least I shall not be alone, without a soul to speak to, or advise with, or stand by me. I shall not be run in upon and worried like a rat.'

He muttered Edith's name, and clenched his hand. As he crept along, in the shadow of the massive buildings, he set his teeth, and muttered dreadful imprecations on her head, and looked from side to side, as if in search of her. Thus, he stole on to the gate of an inn-yard. The people were a-bed; but his ringing at the bell soon produced a man with a lantern, in company with whom he was presently in a dim coach-house, bargaining for the hire of an old phaeton, to Paris.

The bargain was a short one; and the horses were soon sent for. Leaving word that the carriage was to follow him when they came, he stole away again, beyond the town, past the old ramparts, out on the open road, which seemed to glide away along the dark plain, like a stream.

Whither did it flow? What was the end of it? As he paused, with some such suggestion within him, looking over the gloomy flat where the slender trees marked out the way, again that flight of Death came rushing up, again went on, impetuous and resistless, again was nothing but a horror in his mind, dark as the scene and undefined as its remotest verge.

There was no wind; there was no passing shadow on the deep shade of the night; there was no noise. The city lay behind him, lighted here and there, and starry worlds were hidden by the masonry of spire and roof that hardly made out any shapes against the sky. Dark and lonely distance lay around him everywhere, and the clocks were faintly striking two.

He went forward for what appeared a long time, and a long way; often stopping to listen. At last the ringing of horses' bells greeted his anxious ears. Now softer, and now louder, now inaudible, now ringing very slowly over bad ground, now brisk and merry, it came on; until with a loud shouting and lashing, a shadowy postillion muffled to the eyes, checked his four struggling horses at his side.

'Who goes there! Monsieur?'

'Yes.'

'Monsieur has walked a long way in the dark midnight.'

'No matter. Everyone to his task. Were there any other horses ordered at the Post-house?'

'A thousand devils! – and pardons! other horses? at this hour? No.'

'Listen, my friend. I am much hurried. Let us see how fast we can travel! The faster, the more money there will be to drink. Off we go then! Quick!'

'Halloa! whoop! Halloa! Hi!' Away, at a gallop, over the black landscape, scattering the dust and dirt like spray!

The clatter and commotion echoed to the hurry and discordance of the fugitive's ideas. Nothing clear without, and nothing clear within. Objects flitting past, merging into one another, dimly descried, confusedly lost sight of, gone! Beyond the changing scraps of fence and cottage immediately upon the road, a lowering waste. Beyond the shifting images that rose up in his mind and vanished as they showed themselves, a black expanse of dread and rage and baffled villainy. Occasionally, a sigh of mountain air came from the distant Jura, fading along the plain. Sometimes that rush which was so furious and horrible, again came sweeping through his fancy, passed away, and left a chill upon his blood.

The lamps, gleaming on the medley of horses' heads, jumbled with the shadowy driver, and the fluttering of his cloak, made a thousand indistinct shapes, answering to his thoughts.

Shadows of familiar people, stooping at their desks and books, in their remembered attitudes; strange apparitions of the man whom he was flying from, or of Edith; repetitions in the ringing bells and rolling wheels, of words that had been spoken; confusions of time and place, making last night a month ago, a month ago last night – home now distant beyond hope, now instantly accessible; commotion, discord, hurry, darkness, and confusion in his mind, and all around him. – Hallo! Hi! away at a gallop over the black landscape; dust and dirt flying like spray, the smoking horses snorting and plunging as if each of them were ridden by a demon, away in a frantic triumph on the dark road – whither?

Again the nameless shock comes speeding up, and as it passes, the bells ring in his ears 'whither?' The wheels roar in his ears 'whither?' All the noise and rattle shapes itself into that cry. The lights and shadows dance upon the horses' heads like imps. No stopping now: no slackening! On, on! Away with him upon the dark road wildly!

He could not think to any purpose. He could not separate one subject of reflection from another, sufficiently to dwell upon it, by itself, for a minute at a time. The crash of his project for the gaining of a voluptuous compensation for past restraint; the overthrow of his treachery to one who had been true and generous to him, but whose least proud word and look he had treasured up, at interest, for years – for false and subtle men will always secretly despise and dislike the object upon which they fawn and always resent the payment and receipt of homage that they know to be worthless; these were the themes uppermost in his mind. A lurking rage against the woman who had so entrapped him and avenged herself was always there; crude and misshapen schemes of retaliation upon her, floated in his brain; but nothing was distinct. A hurry and contradiction pervaded all his thoughts. Even while he was so busy with this fevered, ineffectual thinking, his one constant idea was, that he would postpone reflection until some indefinite time.

Then, the old days before the second marriage rose up in his remembrance. He thought how jealous he had been of the boy, how jealous he had been of the girl, how artfully he had kept intruders at a distance, and drawn a circle round his dupe that none but himself should cross; and then he thought, had he done all this to be flying now, like a scared thief, from only the poor dupe?

He could have laid hands upon himself for his cowardice, but it was the very shadow of his defeat, and could not be separated from it. To have his confidence in his own knavery so shattered at a blow – to be within his own knowledge such a miserable tool – was like being paralysed. With an impotent ferocity he raged at Edith, and hated Mr Dombey and hated himself, but still he fled, and could do nothing else.

Again and again he listened for the sound of wheels behind. Again and again his fancy heard it, coming on louder and louder. At last he was so persuaded of this, that he cried out, 'Stop', preferring even the loss of ground to such uncertainty.

The word soon brought carriage, horses, driver, all in a heap together, across the road.

'The devil!' cried the driver, looking over his shoulder, 'what's the matter?'

'Hark! What's that?'

'What?'

'That noise?'

'Ah Heaven, be quiet, cursed brigand!' to a horse who shook his bells 'What noise?'

'Behind.'

'Is it not another carriage at a gallop? There! What's that?'

'Miscreant with a Pig's head, stand still!' to another horse, who bit another, who frightened the other two, who plunged and backed. 'There is nothing coming.'

'Nothing.'

'No, nothing but the day yonder.'

'You are right, I think. I hear nothing now, indeed. Go on!'

The entangled equipage, half hidden in the reeking cloud from the horses, goes on slowly at first, for the driver, checked unnecessarily in his progress, sulkily takes out a pocket-knife, and puts a new lash to his whip. Then 'Hallo, whoop! Hallo, hi!' Away once more, savagely.

And now the stars faded, and the day glimmered, and standing in the carriage, looking back, he could discern the track by which he had come, and see that there was no traveller within view, on all the heavy expanse. And soon it was broad day, and the sun began to shine on cornfields and vineyards; and solitary labourers, risen from little temporary huts by heaps of stones upon the road, were, here and there, at work repairing the highway, or eating bread. By and by, there were peasants going to their daily labour, or to market, or lounging at the doors of poor cottages, gazing idly at him as he passed. And then there was a postyard, ankle-deep in mud, with steaming dunghills and vast outhouses half ruined; and looking on this dainty prospect, an immense, old, shadeless, glaring, stone chateau, with half its windows blinded, and green damp crawling lazily over it, from the balustraded terrace to the taper tips of the extinguishers upon the turrets.

Gathered up moodily in a corner of the carriage, and only intent on going fast – except when he stood up, for a mile together, and looked back; which he would do whenever there was a piece of open country – he went on, still postponing thought indefinitely, and still always tormented with thinking to no purpose.

Shame, disappointment, and discomfiture gnawed at his heart; a constant apprehension of being overtaken, or met – for he was groundlessly afraid even of travellers, who came towards him by the way he was going – oppressed him heavily. The same intolerable awe and dread that had come upon him in the night, returned unweakened in the day. The monotonous ringing of the bells and tramping of the horses; the monotony of his anxiety, and useless rage; the monotonous wheel of fear, regret, and passion, he kept turning round and round; made the journey like a vision, in which nothing was quite real but his own torment.

It was a vision of long roads, that stretched away to an horizon, always receding and never gained; of ill-paved towns, up hill and down, where faces came to dark doors and ill-glazed windows, and where rows of mud-bespattered cows and oxen were tied up for sale in the long narrow streets, butting and lowing, and receiving blows on their blunt heads from bludgeons that might have beaten them in; of bridges, crosses, churches, postyards, new horses being put in against their wills, and the horses of the last stage reeking, panting, and laying their drooping heads together dolefully at stable doors; of little cemeteries with black crosses settled sideways in the graves, and withered wreaths upon them dropping away; again of long, long roads, dragging themselves out, up hill and down, to the treacherous horizon.

Of morning, noon, and sunset; night, and the rising of an early moon.

Of long roads temporarily left behind, and a rough pavement reached; of battering and clattering over it, and looking up, among house-roofs, at a great church-tower; of getting out and eating hastily, and drinking draughts of wine that had no cheering influence; of coming forth afoot, among a host of beggars – blind men with quivering eyelids, led by old women holding candles to their faces; idiot girls; the lame, the epileptic, and the palsied – of passing through the clamour, and looking from his seat at the upturned countenances and outstretched hands, with a hurried dread of recognising some pursuer pressing forward – of galloping away again, upon the long, long road, gathered up, dull and stunned, in his corner, or rising to see where the moon shone faintly on a patch of the same endless road miles away, or looking back to see who followed.

Of never sleeping, but sometimes dozing with unclosed eyes, and springing up with a start, and a reply aloud to an imaginary voice. Of cursing himself for being there, for having fled, for having let her go, for not having confronted and defied him. Of having a deadly quarrel with the whole world, but chiefly with himself. Of blighting everything with his black mood as he was carried on and away.

It was a fevered vision of things past and present all confounded together; of his life and journey blended into one. Of being madly hurried somewhere, whither he must go. Of old scenes starting up among the novelties through which he travelled. Of musing and brooding over what was past and distant, and seeming to take no notice of the actual objects he encountered, but with a wearisome exhausting consciousness of being bewildered by them, and having their images all crowded in his hot brain after they were gone.

A vision of change upon change, and still the same monotony of bells and wheels, and horses' feet, and no rest. Of town and country, postyards, horses, drivers, hill and valley, light and darkness, road and pavement, height and hollow, wet weather and dry, and still the same monotony of bells and wheels, and horses' feet, and no rest. A vision of tending on at last, towards the distant capital, by busier roads, and sweeping round, by old cathedrals, and dashing through small towns and villages, less thinly scattered on the road than formerly, and sitting shrouded in his corner, with his cloak up to his face, as people passing by looked at him.

Of rolling on and on, always postponing thought, and always

racked with thinking; of being unable to reckon up the hours he had been upon the road, or to comprehend the points of time and place in his journey. Of being parched and giddy, and half mad. Of pressing on, in spite of all, as if he could not stop, and coming into Paris, where the turbid river held its swift course undisturbed, between two brawling streams of life and motion.

A troubled vision, then, of bridges, quays, interminable streets; of wine-shops, water-carriers, great crowds of people, soldiers, coaches, military drums, arcades. Of the monotony of bells and wheels and horses' feet being at length lost in the universal din and uproar. Of the gradual subsidence of that noise as he passed out in another carriage by a different barrier from that by which he had entered. Of the restoration, as he travelled on towards the seacoast, of the monotony of bells and wheels, and horses' feet, and no rest.

Of sunset once again, and nightfall. Of long roads again, and dead of night, and feeble lights in windows by the roadside; and still the old monotony of bells and wheels, and horses' feet, and no rest. Of dawn, and daybreak, and the rising of the sun. Of tolling slowly up a hill, and feeling on its top the fresh sea-breeze; and seeing the morning light upon the edges of the distant waves. Of coming down into a harbour when the tide was at its full, and seeing fishing-boats float on, and glad women and children waiting for them. Of nets and seamen's clothes spread out to dry upon the shore; of busy sailors, and their voices high among ships' masts and rigging; of the buoyancy and brightness of the water, and the universal sparkling.

Of receding from the coast, and looking back upon it from the deck when it was a haze upon the water, with here and there a little opening of bright land where the Sun struck. Of the swell, and flash, and murmur of the calm sea. Of another grey line on the ocean, on the vessel's track, fast growing clearer and higher. Of cliffs and buildings, and a windmill, and a church, becoming more and more visible upon it. Of steaming on at last into smooth water, and mooring to a pier whence groups of people looked down, greeting friends on board. Of disembarking, passing among them quickly, shunning every one; and of being at last again in England.

He had thought, in his dream, of going down into a remote country-place he knew, and lying quiet there, while he secretly informed himself of what transpired, and determined how to act, Still in the same stunned condition, he remembered a certain station on the railway, where he would have to branch off to his place of destination, and where there was a quiet Inn. Here, he indistinctly resolved to tarry and rest.

With this purpose he slunk into a railway carriage as quickly as he could, and lying there wrapped in his cloak as if he were asleep, was soon borne far away from the sea, and deep into the inland green. Arrived at his destination he looked out, and surveyed it carefully. He was not mistaken in his impression of the place. It was a retired spot, on the borders of a little wood. Only one house, newly-built or altered for the purpose, stood there, surrounded by its neat garden; the small town that was nearest, was some miles away. Here he alighted then; and going straight into the tavern, unobserved by anyone, secured two rooms upstairs communicating with each other, and sufficiently retired.

His object was to rest, and recover the command of himself, and the balance of his mind. Imbecile discomfiture and rage – so that, as he walked about his room, he ground his teeth – had complete possession of him. His thoughts, not to be stopped or directed, still wandered where they would, and dragged him after them. He was stupefied, and he was wearied to death.

But, as if there were a curse upon him that he should never rest again, his drowsy senses would not lose their consciousness. He had no more influence with them, in this regard, than if they had been another man's. It was not that they forced him to take note of present sounds and objects, but that they would not be diverted from the whole hurried vision of his journey. It was constantly before him all at once.

She stood there, with her dark disdainful eyes again upon him; and he was riding on nevertheless, through town and country, light and darkness, wet weather and dry, over road and pavement, hill and valley, height and hollow, jaded and scared by the monotony of bells and wheels, and horses' feet, and no rest.

'What day is this?' he asked of the waiter, who was making preparations for his dinner.

'Day, Sir?'

'Is it Wednesday?'

'Wednesday, Sir? No, Sir. Thursday, Sir.'

'I forgot. How goes the time? My watch is unwound.'

'Wants a few minutes of five o'clock, Sir. Been travelling a long time, Sir, perhaps?'

'Yes.'

'By rail, Sir?'

'Yes.'

'Very confusing, Sir. Not much in the habit of travelling by rail myself, Sir, but gentlemen frequently say so.'

'Do many gentlemen come here?

'Pretty well, Sir, in general. Nobody here at present. Rather slack just now, Sir. Everything is slack, Sir.'

He made no answer; but had risen into a sitting posture on the sofa where he had been lying, and leaned forward with an arm on each knee, staring at the ground. He could not master his own attention for a minute together. It rushed away where it would, but it never, for an instant, lost itself in sleep.

He drank a quantity of wine after dinner, in vain. No such artificial means would bring sleep to his eyes. His thoughts, more incoherent, dragged him more unmercifully after them – as if a wretch, condemned to such expiation, were drawn at the heels of wild horses. No oblivion, and no rest.

How long he sat, drinking and brooding, and being dragged in imagination hither and thither, no one could have told less correctly than he. But he knew that he had been sitting a long time by candle-light, when he started up and listened, in a sudden terror.

For now, indeed, it was no fancy. The ground shook, the house rattled, the fierce impetuous rush was in the air! He felt it come up, and go darting by; and even when he had hurried to the window, and saw what it was, he stood, shrinking from it, as if it were not safe to look.

A curse upon the fiery devil, thundering along so smoothly, tracked through the distant valley by a glare of light and lurid smoke, and gone! He felt as if he had been plucked out of its path, and saved from being torn asunder. It made him shrink and shudder even now, when its faintest hum was hushed, and when the lines of iron road he could trace in the moonlight, running to a point, were as empty and as silent as a desert.

Unable to rest, and irresistibly attracted — or he thought so — to this road, he went out, and lounged on the brink of it, marking the way the train had gone, by the yet smoking cinders that were lying in its track. After a lounge of some half hour in the direction by which it had disappeared, he turned and walked the other way — still keeping to the brink of the road — past the inn garden, and a long way down; looking curiously at the bridges, signals, lamps, and wondering when another Devil would come by.

A trembling of the ground, and quick vibration in his ears; a dis-tant shriek; a dull light advancing, quickly changed to two red eyes, and a fierce fire, dropping glowing coals; an irresistible bearing on of a great roaring and dilating mass; a high wind, and a rattle — another come and gone, and he holding to a gate, as if to save himself!

He waited for another, and for another.

He walked back to his former point, and back again to that, and still, through the wearisome vision of his journey, looked for these approaching monsters. He loitered about the station, waiting until one should stay to call there; and when one did, and was detached for water, he stood parallel with it, watching its heavy wheels and brazen front, and thinking what a cruel power and might it had. Ugh! To see the great wheels slowly turning, and to think of being run down and crushed!

Disordered with wine and want of rest – that want which nothing, although he was so weary, would appease – these ideas and objects assumed a diseased importance in his thoughts. When he went back to his room, which was not until near midnight, they still haunted him, and he sat listening for the coming of another.

So in his bed, whither he repaired with no hope of sleep. He still lay listening; and when he felt the trembling and vibration, got up and went to the window, to watch (as he could from its position) the dull light changing to the two red eyes, and the fierce fire dropping glowing coals, and the rush of the giant as it fled past, and the track of glare and smoke along the valley. Then he would glance in the direction by which he intended to depart at sunrise, as there was no rest for him there; and would lie down again, to be troubled by the vision of his journey, and the old monotony of bells and wheels and horses' feet, until another came. This lasted all night. So far from resuming the mastery of himself, he seemed, if possible, to lose it more and more, as the night crept on. When the dawn appeared, he was still tormented with thinking, still postponing thought until he should be in a better state; the past, present, and future all floated confusedly before him, and he had lost all power of looking steadily at any one of them.

'At what time,' he asked the man who had waited on him overnight, now entering with a candle, 'do I leave here, did you say?'

'About a quarter after four, Sir. Express comes through at four, Sir. – It don't stop.'

He passed his hand across his throbbing head, and looked at his watch. Nearly half-past three.

'Nobody going with you, Sir, probably,' observed the man. 'Two gentlemen here, Sir, but they're waiting for the train to London.'

'I thought you said there was nobody here,' said Carker, turning upon him with the ghost of his old smile, when he was angry or suspicious.

'Not then, sir. Two gentlemen came in the night by the short train that stops here, Sir. Warm water, Sir?'

'No; and take away the candle. There's day enough for me.'

Having thrown himself upon the bed, half-dressed he was at the window as the man left the room. The cold light of morning had succeeded to night and there was already, in the sky, the red suffusion of the coming sun. He bathed his head and face with water – there was no cooling influence in it for him – hurriedly put on his clothes, paid what he owed, and went out.

The air struck chill and comfortless as it breathed upon him. There was a heavy dew; and, hot as he was, it made him shiver. After a glance at the place where he had walked last night, and at the signal-lights burning in the morning, and bereft of their significance, he turned to where the sun was rising, and beheld it, in its glory, as it broke upon the scene.

So awful, so transcendent in its beauty, so divinely solemn.

As he cast his faded eyes upon it, where it rose, tranquil and serene, unmoved by all the wrong and wickedness on which its beams had shone since the beginning of the world, who shall say that some weak sense of virtue upon Earth, and its in Heaven, did not manifest itself, even to him? If ever he remembered sister or brother with a touch of tenderness and remorse, who shall say it was not then?

He needed some such touch then. Death was on him. He was marked off – the living world, and going down into his grave.

He paid the money for his journey to the country-place he had thought of; and was walking to and fro, alone, looking along the lines of iron, across the valley in one direction, and towards a dark bridge near at hand in the other; when, turning in his walk, where it was bounded by one end of the wooden stage on which he paced up and down, he saw the man from whom he had fled, emerging from the door by which he himself had entered.

And their eyes met.

In the quick unsteadiness of the surprise, he staggered, and slipped on to the road below him. But recovering his feet immediately, he stepped back a pace or two upon that road, to interpose some wider space between them, and looked at his pursuer, breathing short and quick.

He heard a shout — another — saw the face change from its vindictive passion to a faint sickness and terror — felt the earth tremble — knew in a moment that the rush was come — uttered a shriek — looked round — saw the red eyes, bleared and dim, in the daylight, close upon him — was beaten down, caught up, and whirled away upon a jagged mill, that spun him round and round, and struck him limb from limb, and licked his stream of life up with its fiery heat, and cast his mutilated fragments in the air.

When the traveller, who had been recognised, recovered from a swoon, he saw them bringing from a distance something covered, that lay heavy and still, upon a board, between four men, and saw that others drove some dogs away that sniffed upon the road, and soaked his blood up, with a train of ashes.

We return to *Mugby Junction* for Dickens's self-contained ghost story, 'The Signal-Man'. By the time it appeared as the Christmas story in *All the Year Round* for 1866, Dickens had experienced the railway disaster at Staplehurst, which appears in the next chapter. There is also thought to be a connection between this eerie tale of a railway accident and the Clayton Tunnel rail crash of 1861. Dickens prepared a public reading version of this story but never performed it, unlike the readings he prepared from 'Barbox Brothers' and 'The Boy at Mugby', which were performed in January and February 1867.

'The Signal-Man' has come to be recognised as a classic ghost story, and is often anthologised alongside the work of other masters of the genre such as M. R. James, Sheridan LeFanu and H. P. Lovecraft. It was successfully adapted for television in 1976, the first Dickens adaptation by Andrew Davies, and is included here in its entirety.

The Signal-Man

'Halloa! Below there!'

When he heard a voice thus calling to him, he was standing at the door of his box, with a flag in his hand, furled round its short pole. One would have thought, considering the nature of the ground, that he could not have doubted from what quarter the voice came; but instead of looking up to where I stood on the top of the steep cutting nearly over his head, he turned himself about, and looked down the Line. There was something remarkable in his manner of doing so, though I could not have said for my life what. But I know it was remarkable enough to attract my notice, even though his figure was foreshortened and shadowed, down in the deep trench, and mine was high above him, so steeped in the glow of an angry sunset, that I had shaded my eyes with my hand before I saw him at all.

'Halloa! Below!'

From looking down the Line, he turned himself about again, and, raising his eyes, saw my figure high above him.

'Is there any path by which I can come down and speak to you?'

He looked up at me without replying, and I looked down at him without pressing him too soon with a repetition of my idle question. Just then there came a vague vibration in the earth and air, quickly changing into a violent pulsation, and an oncoming rush that caused me to start back, as though it had force to draw me down. When such vapour as rose to my height from this rapid train had passed me, and was skimming away over the landscape, I looked down again, and saw him refurling the flag he had shown while the train went by.

I repeated my inquiry. After a pause, during which he seemed to regard me with fixed attention, he motioned with his rolled-up flag towards a point on my level, some two or three hundred yards distant. I called down to him, 'All right!' and made for that point. There, by dint of looking closely about me, I found a rough zigzag descending path notched out, which I followed.

The cutting was extremely deep, and unusually precipitate. It was made through a clammy stone, that became oozier and wetter as I went down. For these reasons, I found the way long enough to give me time to recall a singular air of reluctance or compulsion with which he had pointed out the path.

When I came down low enough upon the zigzag descent to see him again, I saw that he was standing between the rails on the way by which the train had lately passed, in an attitude as if he were waiting for me to appear. He had his left hand at his chin, and that left elbow rested on his right hand, crossed over his breast. His attitude was one of such expectation and watchfulness that I stopped a moment, wondering at it.

I resumed my downward way, and stepping out upon the level of the railroad, and drawing nearer to him, saw that he was a dark sallow man, with a dark beard and rather heavy eyebrows. His post was in as solitary and dismal a place as ever I saw. On either side, a dripping-wet wall of jagged stone, excluding all view but a strip of sky; the perspective one way only a crooked prolongation of this great dungeon; the shorter perspective in the other direction terminating in a gloomy red light, and the gloomier entrance to a black tunnel, in whose massive architecture there was a barbarous, depressing, and forbidding air.

So little sunlight ever found its way to this spot, that it had an earthy, deadly smell; and so much cold wind rushed through it, that it struck chill to me, as if I had left the natural world.

Before he stirred, I was near enough to him to have touched him. Not even then removing his eyes from mine, he stepped back one step, and lifted his hand.

This was a lonesome post to occupy (I said), and it had riveted my attention when I looked down from up yonder. A visitor was a rarity, I should suppose; not an unwelcome rarity, I hoped? In me, he merely saw a man who had been shut up within narrow limits all his life, and who, being at last set free, had a newly-awakened interest in these great works. To such purpose I spoke to him; but I am far from sure of the terms I used; for, besides that I am not happy in opening any conversation, there was something in the man that daunted me.

He directed a most curious look towards the red light near the tunnel's mouth, and looked all about it, as if something were missing from it, and then looked at me.

That light was part of his charge? Was it not?

He answered in a low voice, – 'Don't you know it is?'

The monstrous thought came into my mind, as I perused the fixed eyes and the saturnine face, that this was a spirit, not a man. I have speculated since, whether there may have been infection in his mind.

In my turn, I stepped back. But in making the action, I detected in his eyes some latent fear of me. This put the monstrous thought to flight.

'You look at me,' I said, forcing a smile, 'as if you had a dread of me.'

'I was doubtful,' he returned, 'whether I had seen you before.'

'Where?'

He pointed to the red light he had looked at.

'There?' I said.

Intently watchful of me, he replied (but without sound), 'Yes.'

'My good fellow, what should I do there? However, be that as it may, I never was there, you may swear.'

'I think I may,' he rejoined. 'Yes; I am sure I may.'

His manner cleared, like my own. He replied to my remarks with readiness, and in well-chosen words. Had he much to do there? Yes; that was to say, he had enough responsibility to bear; but exactness and watchfulness were what was required of him, and of actual work – manual labour – he had next to none. To change that signal, to trim those lights, and to turn this iron handle now and then, was all he had to do under that head. Regarding those many long and lonely hours of which I seemed to make so much, he could only say that the routine of his life had shaped itself into that form, and he had grown used to it. He had taught himself a language down here, – if only to know it by sight, and to have formed his own crude ideas of its pronunciation, could be called learning it. He had also worked at fractions and decimals, and tried a little algebra; but he was, and had been as a boy, a poor hand at figures. Was it necessary for him when on duty always to remain in that channel of damp air, and could he never rise into the sunshine from between those high stone walls? Why, that depended upon times and circumstances. Under some conditions there would be less upon the Line than under others, and the same held good as to certain hours of the day and night.

In bright weather, he did choose occasions for getting a little above these lower shadows; but, being at all times liable to be called by his electric bell, and at such times listening for it with redoubled anxiety, the relief was less than I would suppose.

He took me into his box, where there was a fire, a desk for an official book in which he had to make certain entries, a telegraphic instrument with its dial, face, and needles, and the little bell of which he had spoken. On my trusting that he would excuse the remark that he had been well educated, and (I hoped I might say without offence) perhaps educated above that station, he observed that instances of slight incongruity in such wise would rarely be found wanting among large bodies of men; that he had heard it was so in work-houses, in the police force, even in that last desperate resource, the army; and that he knew it was so, more or less, in any great railway staff. He had been, when young (if I could believe it, sitting in that hut, – he scarcely could), a student of natural philosophy, and had attended lectures; but he had run wild, misused his opportunities, gone down, and never risen again. He had no complaint to offer about that. He had made his bed, and he lay upon it. It was far too late to make another.

All that I have here condensed he said in a quiet manner, with his grave dark regards divided between me and the fire. He threw in the word, 'Sir', from time to time, and especially when he referred to his youth, – as though to request me to understand that he claimed to be nothing but what I found him. He was several times interrupted by the little bell, and had to read off messages, and send replies. Once he had to stand without the door, and display a flag as a train passed, and make some verbal communication to the driver. In the discharge of his duties, I observed him to be remarkably exact and vigilant, breaking off his discourse at a syllable, and remaining silent until what he had to do was done.

In a word, I should have set this man down as one of the safest of men to be employed in that capacity, but for the circumstance that while he was speaking to me he twice broke off with a fallen colour, turned his face towards the little bell when it did NOT ring, opened the door of the hut (which was kept shut to exclude the unhealthy damp), and looked out towards the red light near the mouth of the tunnel. On both of those occasions, he came back to the fire with the inexplicable air upon him which I had remarked, without being able to define, when we were so far asunder.

Said I, when I rose to leave him, 'You almost make me think that I have met with a contented man.'

(I am afraid I must acknowledge that I said it to lead him on.)

'I believe I used to be so,' he rejoined, in the low voice in which he had first spoken; 'but I am troubled, sir, I am troubled.'

He would have recalled the words if he could. He had said them, however, and I took them up quickly.

'With what? What is your trouble?'

'It is very difficult to impart, sir. It is very, very difficult to speak of. If ever you make me another visit, I will try to tell you.'

'But I expressly intend to make you another visit. Say, when shall it be?'

'I go off early in the morning, and I shall be on again at ten to-morrow night, sir.'

'I will come at eleven.'

He thanked me, and went out at the door with me. 'I'll show my white light, sir,' he said, in his peculiar low voice, 'till you have found the way up. When you have found it, don't call out! And when you are at the top, don't call out!'

His manner seemed to make the place strike colder to me, but I said no more than, 'Very well'.

'And when you come down to-morrow night, don't call out! Let me ask you a parting question. What made you cry, "Halloa! Below there!" to-night?'

'Heaven knows,' said I. 'I cried something to that effect –'

'Not to that effect, sir. Those were the very words. I know them well.'

'Admit those were the very words. I said them, no doubt, because I saw you below.'

'For no other reason?'

'What other reason could I possibly have?'

'You had no feeling that they were conveyed to you in any super-natural way?'

'No.'

He wished me good-night, and held up his light. I walked by the side of the down Line of rails (with a very disagreeable sensation of a train coming behind me) until I found the path. It was easier to mount than to descend, and I got back to my inn without any adventure.

Punctual to my appointment, I placed my foot on the first notch of the zigzag next night, as the distant clocks were striking eleven. He was waiting for me at the bottom, with his white light on. 'I have not called out,' I said, when we came close together; 'may I speak now?'

'By all means, sir.'

'Good-night, then, and here's my hand.'

'Good-night, sir, and here's mine.' With that we walked side by side to his box, entered it, closed the door, and sat down by the fire.

'I have made up my mind, sir,' he began, bending forward as soon as we were seated, and speaking in a tone but a little above a whisper, 'that you shall not have to ask me twice what troubles me. I took you for someone else yesterday evening. That troubles me.'

'That mistake?'

'No. That someone else.'

'Who is it?'

'I don't know.'

'Like me?'

'I don't know. I never saw the face. The left arm is across the face, and the right arm is waved, – violently waved. This way.'

I followed his action with my eyes, and it was the action of an arm gesticulating, with the utmost passion and vehemence, 'For God's sake, clear the way!'

'One moonlight night,' said the man, 'I was sitting here, when I heard a voice cry, "Halloa! Below there!" I started up, looked from that door, and saw this Someone else standing by the red light near the tunnel, waving as I just now showed you. The voice seemed hoarse with shouting, and it cried, "Look out! Look out!" And then again, "Halloa! Below there! Look out!" I caught up my lamp, turned it on red, and ran towards the figure, calling, "What's wrong? What has happened? Where?" It stood just outside the blackness of the tunnel. I advanced so close upon it that I wondered at its keeping the sleeve across its eyes. I ran right up at it, and had my hand stretched out to pull the sleeve away, when it was gone.'

'Into the tunnel?' said I.

'No. I ran on into the tunnel, five hundred yards. I stopped, and held my lamp above my head, and saw the figures of the measured distance, and saw the wet stains stealing down the walls and trickling through the arch. I ran out again faster than I had run in (for I had a mortal abhorrence of the place upon me), and I looked all round the red light with my own red light, and I went up the iron ladder to the gallery atop of it, and I came down again, and ran back here. I telegraphed both ways, "An alarm has been given. Is anything wrong?" The answer came back, both ways, "All well."'

Resisting the slow touch of a frozen finger tracing out my spine, I showed him how that this figure must be a deception of his sense of sight; and how that figures, originating in disease of the delicate nerves that minister to the functions of the eye, were known to have often troubled patients, some of whom had become conscious of the nature of their affliction, and had even proved it by experiments upon themselves. 'As to an imaginary cry,' said I, 'do but listen for a moment to the wind in this unnatural valley while we speak so low, and to the wild harp it makes of the telegraph wires.'

That was all very well, he returned, after we had sat listening for a while, and he ought to know something of the wind and the wires, – he who so often passed long winter nights there, alone and watching. But he would beg to remark that he had not finished.

I asked his pardon, and he slowly added these words, touching my arm:

'Within six hours after the Appearance, the memorable accident on this Line happened, and within ten hours the dead and wounded were brought along through the tunnel over the spot where the figure had stood.'

A disagreeable shudder crept over me, but I did my best against it. It was not to be denied, I rejoined, that this was a remarkable coincidence, calculated deeply to impress his mind. But it was unquestionable that remarkable coincidences did continually occur, and they must be taken into account in dealing with such a subject. Though to be sure I must admit, I added (for I thought I saw that he was going to bring the objection to bear upon me), men of common sense did not allow much for coincidences in making the ordinary calculations of life.

He again begged to remark that he had not finished.

I again begged his pardon for being betrayed into interruptions.

'This,' he said, again laying his hand upon my arm, and glancing over his shoulder with hollow eyes, 'was just a year ago. Six or seven months passed, and I had recovered from the surprise and shock, when one morning, as the day was breaking, I, standing at the door, looked towards the red light, and saw the spectre again.' He stopped, with a fixed look at me.

'Did it cry out?'

'No. It was silent.'

'Did it wave its arm?'

'No. It leaned against the shaft of the light, with both hands before the face. Like this.'

Once more I followed his action with my eyes. It was an action of mourning. I have seen such an attitude in stone figures on tombs.

'Did you go up to it?'

'I came in and sat down, partly to collect my thoughts, partly because it had turned me faint. When I went to the door again, daylight was above me, and the ghost was gone.'

'But nothing followed? Nothing came of this?'

He touched me on the arm with his forefinger twice or thrice giving a ghastly nod each time:

'That very day, as a train came out of the tunnel, I noticed, at a carriage window on my side, what looked like a confusion of hands and heads, and something waved. I saw it just in time to signal the driver, Stop! He shut off, and put his brake on, but the train drifted past here a hundred and fifty yards or more. I ran after it, and, as I went along, heard terrible screams and cries. A beautiful young lady had died instantaneously in one of the compartments, and was brought in here, and laid down on this floor between us.'

Involuntarily I pushed my chair back, as I looked from the boards at which he pointed to himself.

'True, sir. True. Precisely as it happened, so I tell it you.'

I could think of nothing to say, to any purpose, and my mouth was very dry. The wind and the wires took up the story with a long lamenting wail.

He resumed. 'Now, sir, mark this, and judge how my mind is troubled. The spectre came back a week ago. Ever since, it has been there, now and again, by fits and starts.'

'At the light?'

'At the Danger-light.'

'What does it seem to do?'

He repeated, if possible with increased passion and vehemence, that former gesticulation of, 'For God's sake, clear the way!'

Then he went on. 'I have no peace or rest for it. It calls to me, for many minutes together, in an agonised manner, "Below there! Look out! Look out!" It stands waving to me. It rings my little bell —'

I caught at that. 'Did it ring your bell yesterday evening when I was here, and you went to the door?'

'Twice.'

'Why, see,' said I, 'how your imagination misleads you. My eyes were on the bell, and my ears were open to the bell, and if I am a living man, it did NOT ring at those times. No, nor at any other time, except when it was rung in the natural course of physical things by the station communicating with you.'

He shook his head. 'I have never made a mistake as to that yet, sir. I have never confused the spectre's ring with the man's. The ghost's ring is a strange vibration in the bell that it derives from nothing else, and I have not asserted that the bell stirs to the eye. I don't wonder that you failed to hear it. But I heard it.'

'And did the spectre seem to be there, when you looked out?'

'It WAS there.'

'Both times?'

He repeated firmly: 'Both times.'

'Will you come to the door with me, and look for it now?'

He bit his under lip as though he were somewhat unwilling, but arose. I opened the door, and stood on the step, while he stood in the doorway. There was the Danger-light. There was the dismal mouth of the tunnel. There were the high, wet stone walls of the cutting. There were the stars above them.

'Do you see it?' I asked him, taking particular note of his face. His eyes were prominent and strained, but not very much more so, perhaps, than my own had been when I had directed them earnestly towards the same spot.

'No,' he answered. 'It is not there.'

'Agreed,' said I.

We went in again, shut the door, and resumed our seats. I was thinking how best to improve this advantage, if it might be called one, when he took up the conversation in such a matter-of-course way, so assuming that there could be no serious question of fact between us, that I felt myself placed in the weakest of positions.

'By this time you will fully understand, sir,' he said, 'that what troubles me so dreadfully is the question, What does the spectre mean?'

I was not sure, I told him, that I did fully understand.

'What is its warning against?' he said, ruminating, with his eyes on the fire, and only by times turning them on me.

'What is the danger? Where is the danger? There is danger overhanging somewhere on the Line. Some dreadful calamity will happen. It is not to be doubted this third time, after what has gone before. But surely this is a cruel haunting of me. What can I do?'

He pulled out his handkerchief, and wiped the drops from his heated forehead.

'If I telegraph Danger, on either side of me, or on both, I can give no reason for it,' he went on, wiping the palms of his hands. 'I should get into trouble, and do no good. They would think I was mad. This is the way it would work, – Message: 'Danger! Take care!' Answer: 'What Danger? Where?' Message: 'Don't know. But, for God's sake, take care!' They would displace me. What else could they do?'

His pain of mind was most pitiable to see. It was the mental torture of a conscientious man, oppressed beyond endurance by an unintelligible responsibility involving life.

'When it first stood under the Danger-light,' he went on, putting his dark hair back from his head, and drawing his hands outward across and across his temples in an extremity of feverish distress, 'why not tell me where that accident was to happen, – if it must happen? Why not tell me how it could be averted, – if it could have been averted? When on its second coming it hid its face, why not tell me, instead, "She is going to die. Let them keep her at home"? If it came, on those two occasions, only to show me that its warnings were true, and so to prepare me for the third, why not warn me plainly now? And I, Lord help me! A mere poor signalman on this solitary station! Why not go to somebody with credit to be believed, and power to act?'

When I saw him in this state, I saw that for the poor man's sake, as well as for the public safety, what I had to do for the time was to compose his mind. Therefore, setting aside all question of reality or unreality between us, I represented to him that whoever thoroughly discharged his duty must do well, and that at least it was his comfort that he understood his duty, though he did not understand these confounding Appearances. In this effort I succeeded far better than in the attempt to reason him out of his conviction. He became calm; the occupations incidental to his post as the night advanced began to make larger demands on his attention: and I left him at two in the morning. I had offered to stay through the night, but he would not hear of it.

That I more than once looked back at the red light as I ascended the pathway, that I did not like the red light, and that I should have slept but poorly if my bed had been under it, I see no reason to conceal. Nor did I like the two sequences of the accident and the dead girl. I see no reason to conceal that either.

But what ran most in my thoughts was the consideration how ought I to act, having become the recipient of this disclosure? I had proved the man to be intelligent, vigilant, painstaking, and exact; but how long might he remain so, in his state of mind? Though in a subordinate position, still he held a most important trust, and would I (for instance) like to stake my own life on the chances of his continuing to execute it with precision?

Unable to overcome a feeling that there would be something treacherous in my communicating what he had told me to his superiors in the Company, without first being plain with himself and proposing a middle course to him, I ultimately resolved to offer to accompany him (otherwise keeping his secret for the present) to the wisest medical practitioner we could hear of in those parts, and to take his opinion. A change in his time of duty would come round next night, he had apprised me, and he would be off an hour or two after sunrise, and on again soon after sunset. I had appointed to return accordingly.

Next evening was a lovely evening, and I walked out early to enjoy it. The sun was not yet quite down when I traversed the field-path near the top of the deep cutting. I would extend my walk for an hour, I said to myself, half an hour on and half an hour back, and it would then be time to go to my signalman's box.

Before pursuing my stroll, I stepped to the brink, and mechanically looked down, from the point from which I had first seen him. I cannot describe the thrill that seized upon me, when, close at the mouth of the tunnel, I saw the appearance of a man, with his left sleeve across his eyes, passionately waving his right arm.

The nameless horror that oppressed me passed in a moment, for in a moment I saw that this appearance of a man was a man indeed, and that there was a little group of other men, standing at a short distance, to whom he seemed to be rehearsing the gesture he made. The Danger-light was not yet lighted. Against its shaft, a little low hut, entirely new to me, had been made of some wooden supports and tarpaulin. It looked no bigger than a bed.

With an irresistible sense that something was wrong, – with a flashing self-reproachful fear that fatal mischief had come of my leaving the man there, and causing no one to be sent to overlook or correct what he did, – I descended the notched path with all the speed I could make.

'What is the matter?' I asked the men.

'Signalman killed this morning, sir.'

'Not the man belonging to that box?'

'Yes, sir.'

'Not the man I know?'

'You will recognise him, sir, if you knew him,' said the man who spoke for the others, solemnly uncovering his own head, and raising an end of the tarpaulin, 'for his face is quite composed.'

'O, how did this happen, how did this happen?' I asked, turning from one to another as the hut closed in again.

'He was cut down by an engine, sir. No man in England knew his work better. But somehow he was not clear of the outer rail. It was just at broad day. He had struck the light, and had the lamp in his hand. As the engine came out of the tunnel, his back was towards her, and she cut him down. That man drove her, and was showing how it happened. Show the gentleman, Tom.'

The man, who wore a rough dark dress, stepped back to his former place at the mouth of the tunnel.

'Coming round the curve in the tunnel, sir,' he said, 'I saw him at the end, like as if I saw him down a perspective-glass. There was no time to check speed, and I knew him to be very careful. As he didn't seem to take heed of the whistle, I shut it off when we were running down upon him, and called to him as loud as I could call.'

'What did you say?'

'I said, 'Below there! Look out! Look out! For God's sake, clear the way!''

I started.

'Ah! it was a dreadful time, sir. I never left off calling to him. I put this arm before my eyes not to see, and I waved this arm to the last; but it was no use.'

Without prolonging the narrative to dwell on any one of its curious circumstances more than on any other, I may, in closing it, point out the coincidence that the warning of the Engine-Driver included, not only the words which the unfortunate signalman had repeated to me as haunting him, but also the words which I myself – not he – had attached, and that only in my own mind, to the gesticulation he had imitated.

9

DANGER AND DISASTER: IN LIFE

CHARLES DICKENS RELIEVING THE SUFFERERS AT THE FATAL RAILWAY ACCIDENT, NEAR STAPLEHURST.—SEE "GOSSIPER," PAGE 84.

On 9 June 1865 Charles Dickens had been returning from France on the tidal express which had left Paris at 7 a.m. He had taken the cross-channel ferry at Boulogne, and resumed the train journey at Folkestone at 2.38 p.m. on its way to Charing Cross. Work was being undertaken on the line between Staplehurst and Headcorn, on the bridge over the River Beult, and rails had been removed. The foreman in charge of the work had consulted the wrong timetable and was not expecting a train for another two hours. The train had been travelling at 50 miles per hour on a downward gradient, and the sight of the danger signal (a man waving a red flag some 500 yards from the site of the work) succeeded in slowing it to a speed of 20 to 30 mph.

The train jumped the 42-foot gap, swerved off the track and broke in two. Seven carriages plunged into the river; the others remained poised over the gap. There were 110 passengers, of whom ten were killed and 14 badly injured. Dickens worked hard to tend the injured and dying, and returned to the carriage to rescue the manuscript of the next instalment of *Our Mutual Friend*, on which he was currently working. He had been accompanied by his mistress, Ellen Ternan, and her mother. Five years later, in 1870, Charles Dickens was himself to die on the same date, 9 June.

Even well before the Staplehurst accident Dickens had been preoccupied for years by the incompetence that was causing deaths on the railways. Between April 1850 and

December 1855, he informed the readers of *Household Words* of the number of people killed or injured in railway accidents in monthly issues of a factual digest called the *Household Narrative of Current Events*. This publication, principally compiled by Dickens's father-in-law George Hogarth, is a compilation of facts and figures, from which we learn, for example, that in the half-year ended 31 December 1851, the number of individual journeys taken on the railway was 47,509,392. Of these 113 ended in fatalities, with a further 264 injured.

There is much correspondence from Dickens to his friends about the Staplehurst incident, but the fullest is this, to Thomas Mitton, his friend and solicitor, on 13 June, the Tuesday after the accident. It is a very powerful and extremely vivid account.

Tuesday, Thirteenth June 1865

My Dear Mitton

I should have written to you yesterday or the day before, if I had been quite up to writing. I am a little shaken, not by the beating and dragging of the carriage in which I was, but by the hard work afterwards in getting out the dying and dead, which was most horrible. I was in the only carriage that did not go over into the stream. It was caught upon the turn by some of the ruin of the bridge, and hung suspended and balanced in an apparently impossible manner. Two ladies were my fellow passengers; an old one, and a young one.

This is exactly what passed: – you may judge from it the precise length of the suspense. Suddenly we were off the rail and beating the ground as the car of a half-emptied balloon might. The old lady cried out 'My God!' and the young one screamed. I caught hold of them both (the old lady sat opposite, and the young one on my left), and said: 'We can't help ourselves, but we can be quiet and composed. Pray don't cry out.' The old lady immediately answered, 'Thank you. Rely upon me. Upon my soul, I will be quiet.' The young lady said in a frantic way, 'Let us join hands and die friends.' We were then all tilted down together in a corner of the carriage, and stopped. I said to them thereupon: 'You may be sure nothing worse can happen. Our danger must be over. Will you remain here without stirring, while I get out of the window?' They both answered quite collectedly, 'Yes,' and I got out without the least notion what had happened. Fortunately I got out with great caution and stood upon the step.

Looking down, I saw the bridge gone and nothing below me but the line of rail. Some people in the two other compartments were madly trying to plunge out at window, and had no idea that there was an open swampy field 15 feet down below them and nothing else! The two guards (one with his face cut) were running up and down on the down side of the bridge (which was not torn up) quite wildly.

I called out to them, 'Look at me. Do stop an instant and look at me, and tell me whether you don't know me.'

One of them answered 'We know you very well, Mr. Dickens.'

'Then,' I said, 'my good fellow for God's sake give me your key, and send one of those labourers here, and I'll empty this carriage.' – We did it quite safely, by means of a plank or two, and when it was done I saw all the rest of the train except the two baggage cars down in the stream. I got into the carriage again for my brandy flask, took off my travelling hat for a basin, climbed down the brickwork, and filled my hat with water.

Suddenly I came upon a staggering man covered with blood (I think he must have been flung clean out of his carriage) with such a frightful cut across the skull that I couldn't bear to look at him. I poured some water over his face, and gave him some to drink, and gave him some brandy, and laid him down on the grass, and he said 'I am gone' and died afterwards.

Then I stumbled over a lady lying on her back against a little pollard tree, with the blood streaming over her face (which was lead colour) in a number of distinct little streams from the head. I asked her if she could swallow a little brandy, and she just nodded, and I gave her some and left her for somebody else. The next time I passed her, she was dead.

Then a man examined at the Inquest yesterday (who evidently

had not the least remembrance of what really passed) came running up to me and implored me to help him find his wife, who was afterwards found dead. No imagination can conceive the ruin of the carriages, or the extraordinary weights under which the people were lying, or the complications into which they were twisted up among iron and wood, and mud and water.

I don't want to be examined at the Inquest, and I don't want to write about it. It could do no good either way, and I could only seem to speak about myself, which, of course I would rather not do. I am keeping very quiet here. I have a – I don't know what to call it – constitutional (I suppose) presence of mind, and was not in the least fluttered at the time. I instantly remembered that I had the MS. of a No. with me, and clambered back into the carriage for it. But in writing these scanty words of recollection I feel the shake and am obliged to stop.

Ever faithfully,
C.D.

Dickens later wrote to his Swiss friend, W.W.F. de Cerjat, on 30 November. 'Lord Campbell's Act' was an 1846 Act only permitting compensation for fatal accidents.

30th November, to W. W. F. de Cerjat

Lastly, a muddle of railways in all directions possible and impossible, with no general public scheme, no general public supervision, enormous waste of money, no fixable responsibility, no accountability but under Lord Campbell's Act. I think of that accident in which I was preserved. Before the most furious and notable train in the twenty-four hours, the head of a gang of workmen takes up the rails. That train changes its time every day as the tide changes, and that head workman is not provided by the railway company with any clock or watch! Lord Shaftesbury wrote to me to ask me what I thought of an obligation on railway companies to put strong walls to all bridges and viaducts. I told him, of course, that the force of such a shock would carry away anything that any company could set up, and I added: 'Ask the minister what he thinks about the votes of the railway interest in the House of Commons, and about his being afraid to lay a finger on it with an eye to his majority.'

The impact of the experience remained with Dickens for the remainder of his life. We find him again writing to de Cerjat on 26 August 1868, shortly after another accident had taken place on 20 August, when an Irish Mail express train, travelling from Euston to Holyhead, collided near Rhyl with a goods train loaded with barrels of petroleum. Thirty-three people were burned to death.

The great subject in England for the moment is the horrible accident to the Irish Mail Train. It is now supposed that the Petroleum (known to be a powerful Anaesthetic) rendered the unfortunate people who were burnt, almost instantly insensible to any sensation. My escape in the great Staplehurst accident of 3 years ago, is not to be obliterated from my nervous system. To this hour I have sudden vague rushes of terror, even when riding in a Hansom Cab, which are perfectly unreasonable, but quite insurmountable. I used to make nothing of driving a pair of horses habitually through the most crowded parts of London. I cannot now drive, with comfort to myself, on the country roads here; and I doubt if I could ride at all in the saddle. My Reading-Secretary and companion knows so well when one of these odd momentary seizures comes upon me in a Railway Carriage, that he instantly produces a dram of brandy, which rallies the blood to the heart and generally prevails. I forget whether I ever told you that my watch (a Chronometer) has never gone exactly, since the accident? – So the Irish catastrophe naturally revives the dreadful things I saw that day.

The original intention of producing this anthology in 2020 was to mark the 150th anniversary of Dickens's death on 9 June 1870, five years to the day since his involvement in the Staplehurst railway accident (see Chapter 9). There is irony in that itself, but also in that, at the time, we had no knowledge of how contemporary rail travel would be so powerfully affected by the coronavirus pandemic.

10

SUSTAINING THE
TRAVELLER

SO LIKELY!

Scene—Bar of a Railway Refreshment Room.

Barmaid. "TEA, SIR?"   Mr. Boozy. "TEA!!! ME!!!!"

Mugby Junction, Dickens's Christmas story for 1864, has already been encountered, and this extract is the final one from it. It demonstrates Dickens's ability to sustain the speech of a character through a substantial piece of writing. It takes its inspiration from one of his experiences on his reading tours. Travelling by train and accompanied by George Dolby, his reading tour manager, and W. H. Wills, his sub-editor on his journals, Dickens visited the refreshment room at Rugby Station while the train halted there because a fire had broken out in one of the carriages. George Dolby gives a well-observed account of the episode in Book 1, Chapter 1 of *Charles Dickens As I Knew Him* (1885).

On this journey a slight accident to the train led to a circumstance which gave Mr Dickens an opportunity for which he had long been looking, to write with the object of improving the commissariat at railway stations, which, it may be within the experience of my readers, was at that time conducted in a most unsatisfactory manner. ... Mr Dickens came along the platform in a state of great excitement, and requested me to accompany him to the refreshment-room. Then, standing in the doorway and pointing with his finger, he described the picture he particularly wished to impress on my mind. 'You see, Dolby – stove to right hand – torn cocoanut matting on floor – counter across room – coffee urn – tea urn – plates of rusks – piles of sawdust sandwiches and shrunken up oranges – bottles – tumblers – and glasses on counter – and *behind* counter, *note particularly*, OUR MISSUS.'

Apparently Dickens's encounter with that formidable figure led to his being refused milk and sugar until he had paid for his coffee.

According to Dolby, Dickens's party was on the way to Manchester and Liverpool, where he was due to deliver readings on 26 April 1866 (Manchester) and 27 and 28 April (Liverpool). 'The Boy at Mugby' appeared at Christmas that year. The six years since the introduction of refreshments for the travelling public seem to have established the characteristic perception of railway catering for many years to come.

The Boy at Mugby

I am the boy at Mugby. That's about what *I* am.

You don't know what I mean? What a pity! But I think you do. I think you must. Look here. I am the boy at what is called The Refreshment Room at Mugby Junction, and what's proudest boast is, that it never yet refreshed a mortal being.

Up in a corner of the Down Refreshment Room at Mugby Junction, in the height of twenty-seven cross draughts (I've often counted 'em while they brush the First-Class hair twenty-seven ways), behind the bottles, among the glasses, bounded on the nor'west by the beer, stood pretty far to the right of a metallic object that's at times the tea-urn and at times the soup-tureen, according to the nature of the last twang imparted to its contents which are the same groundwork, fended off from the traveller by a barrier of stale sponge-cakes erected atop of the counter, and lastly exposed sideways to the glare of Our Missis's eye – you ask a Boy so sitiwated, next time you stop in a hurry at Mugby, for anything to drink; you take particular notice that he'll try to seem not to hear you, that he'll appear in a absent manner to survey the Line through a transparent medium composed of your head and body, and that he won't serve you as long as you can possibly bear it. That's me.

What a lark it is! We are the Model Establishment, we are, at Mugby. Other Refreshment Rooms send their imperfect young ladies up to be finished off by our Missis. For some of the young

ladies, when they're new to the business, come into it mild! Ah!
Our Missis, she soon takes that out of 'em. Why, I originally come
into the business meek myself. But Our Missis, she soon took that
out of *me*.

What a delightful lark it is! I look upon us Refreshmenters as
ockipying the only proudly independent footing on the Line. There's
Papers, for instance, – my honourable friend, if he will allow me
to call him so, – him as belongs to Smith's bookstall. Why, he no
more dares to be up to our Refreshmenting games than he dares to
jump a top of a locomotive with her steam at full pressure, and cut
away upon her alone, driving himself, at limited-mail speed. Papers,
he'd get his head punched at every compartment, first, second, and
third, the whole length of a train, if he was to ventur to imitate my
demeanour. It's the same with the porters, the same with the guards,
the same with the ticket clerks, the same the whole way up to the secretary, traffic-manager, or very chairman. There ain't a one among
'em on the nobly independent footing we are. Did you ever catch
one of them, when you wanted anything of him, making a system
of surveying the Line through a transparent medium composed of
your head and body? I should hope not.

You should see our Bandolining Room at Mugby Junction. It's
led to by the door behind the counter, which you'll notice usually
stands ajar, and it's the room where Our Missis and our young
ladies Bandolines their hair. You should see 'em at it, betwixt trains,
Bandolining away, as if they was anointing themselves for the
combat.

When you're telegraphed, you should see their noses all a-going
up with scorn, as if it was a part of the working of the same Cooke
and Wheatstone electrical machinery. You should hear Our Missis
give the word, 'Here comes the Beast to be Fed!' and then you
should see 'em indignantly skipping across the Line, from the Up
to the Down, or Wicer Warsaw, and begin to pitch the stale pastry
into the plates, and chuck the sawdust sangwiches under the glass

covers, and get out the – ha, ha, ha! – the sherry, – O my eye, my eye! – for your Refreshment.

It's only in the Isle of the Brave and Land of the Free (by which, of course, I mean to say Britannia) that Refreshmenting is so effective, so 'olesome, so constitutional a check upon the public. There was a Foreigner, which having politely, with his hat off, beseeched our young ladies and Our Missis for 'a leetel gloss host prarndee', and having had the Line surveyed through him by all and no other acknowledgment, was a-proceeding at last to help himself, as seems to be the custom in his own country, when Our Missis, with her hair almost a-coming un-Bandolined with rage, and her eyes omitting sparks, flew at him, cotched the decanter out of his hand, and said, 'Put it down! I won't allow that!' The foreigner turned pale, stepped back with his arms stretched out in front of him, his hands clasped, and his shoulders riz, and exclaimed: 'Ah! Is it possible, this! That these disdaineous females and this ferocious old woman are placed here by the administration, not only to empoison the voyagers, but to affront them! Great Heaven! How arrives it? The English people. Or is he then a slave? Or idiot?' Another time, a merry, wideawake American gent had tried the sawdust and spit it out, and had tried the Sherry and spit that out, and had tried in vain to sustain exhausted natur upon Butter-Scotch, and had been rather extra Bandolined and Line-surveyed through, when, as the bell was ringing and he paid Our Missis, he says, very loud and good-tempered: 'I tell Yew what 'tis, ma'arm. I la'af. Theer! I la'af. I Dew. I oughter ha' seen most things, for I hail from the Onlimited side of the Atlantic Ocean, and I haive travelled right slick over the Limited, head on through Jeerusalemm and the East, and likeways France and Italy, Europe Old World, and am now upon the track to the Chief Europian Village; but such an Institution as Yew, and Yewer young ladies, and Yewer fixin's solid and liquid, afore the glorious Tarnal I never did see yet! And if I hain't found the eighth wonder of monarchical Creation, in finding Yew and Yewer young ladies, and Yewer fixin's solid and liquid, all as aforesaid, established in a country where the people air not absolute Loo-naticks, I am Extra Double Darned with a Nip and Frizzle to the innermostest grit! Wheerfur – Theer! – I la'af! I Dew, ma'arm. I la'af!' And so he went, stamping and shaking his sides, along the platform all the way to his own compartment.

I think it was her standing up agin the Foreigner as giv' Our Missis the idea of going over to France, and droring a comparison betwixt Refreshmenting as followed among the frog-eaters, and Refreshmenting as triumphant in the Isle of the Brave and Land of the Free (by which, of course, I mean to say agin, Britannia). Our young ladies, Miss Whiff, Miss Piff, and Mrs Sniff, was unanimous opposed to her going; for, as they says to Our Missis one and all, it is well beknown to the hends of the herth as no other nation except Britain has a idea of anythink, but above all of business. Why then should you tire yourself to prove what is already proved? Our Missis, however (being a teazer at all pints) stood out grim obstinate, and got a return pass by Southeastern Tidal, to go right through, if such should be her dispositions, to Marseilles.

Sniff is husband to Mrs Sniff, and is a regular insignificant cove. He looks arter the sawdust department in a back room, and is sometimes, when we are very hard put to it, let behind the counter with a corkscrew; but never when it can be helped, his demeanour towards the public being disgusting servile. How Mrs Sniff ever come so far to lower herself as to marry him, I don't know; but I suppose he does, and I should think he wished he didn't, for he leads a awful life. Mrs Sniff couldn't be much harder with him if he was public. Similarly, Miss Whiff and Miss Piff, taking the tone of Mrs Sniff, they shoulder Sniff about when he *is* let in with a corkscrew, and they whisk things out of his hands when in his servility he is a-going to let the public have 'em, and they snap him up when in the crawling baseness of his spirit he is a-going to answer a public question, and they drore more tears into his eyes than ever the mustard does which he all day long lays on to the sawdust. (But it ain't strong.) Once, when Sniff had the repulsiveness to reach across to get the milk-pot to hand over for a baby, I see Our Missis in her rage catch him by both his shoulders, and spin him out into the Bandolining Room.

But Mrs Sniff, – how different! She's the one! She's the one as you'll notice to be always looking another way from you, when you look at her. She's the one with the small waist buckled in tight in front, and with the lace cuffs at her wrists, which she puts on the edge of the counter before her, and stands a smoothing while the public foams. This smoothing the cuffs and looking another way while the public foams is the last accomplishment taught to the young ladies as come to Mugby to be finished by Our Missis; and it's always taught by Mrs Sniff.

When Our Missis went away upon her journey, Mrs Sniff was left in charge. She did hold the public in check most beautiful! In all my time, I never see half so many cups of tea given without milk to people as wanted it with, nor half so many cups of tea with milk given to people as wanted it without. When foaming ensued, Mrs Sniff would say: 'Then you'd better settle it among yourselves, and change with one another.' It was a most highly delicious lark. I enjoyed the Refreshmenting business more than ever, and was so glad I had took to it when young.

Our Missis returned. It got circulated among the young ladies, and it as it might be penetrated to me through the crevices of the Bandolining Room, that she had Orrors to reveal, if revelations so contemptible could be dignified with the name. Agitation become awakened. Excitement was up in the stirrups. Expectation stood a-tiptoe. At length it was put forth that on our slacked evening in the week, and at our slackest time of that evening betwixt trains, Our Missis would give her views of foreign Refreshmenting, in the Bandolining Room.

It was arranged tasteful for the purpose.

The Bandolining table and glass was hid in a corner, a arm-chair was elevated on a packing-case for Our Missis's ockypation, a table and a tumbler of water (no sherry in it, thankee) was placed beside it. Two of the pupils, the season being autumn, and hollyhocks and dahlias being in, ornamented the wall with three devices in those flowers. On one might be read, 'MAY ALBION NEVER LEARN;' on another 'KEEP THE PUBLIC DOWN;' on another, 'OUR REFRESHMENTING CHARTER.' The whole had a beautiful appearance, with which the beauty of the sentiments corresponded.

On Our Missis's brow was wrote Severity, as she ascended the fatal platform. (Not that that was anythink new.) Miss Whiff and Miss Piff sat at her feet. Three chairs from the Waiting Room might have been perceived by a average eye, in front of her, on which the pupils was accommodated. Behind them a very close observer might have discerned a Boy. Myself.

'Where,' said Our Missis, glancing gloomily around, 'is Sniff?'

'I thought it better,' answered Mrs Sniff, 'that he should not be let to come in. He is such an Ass.'

'No doubt,' assented Our Missis. 'But for that reason is it not desirable to improve his mind?'

'Oh, nothing will ever improve *him*,' said Mrs Sniff.

'However', pursued Our Missis, 'call him in, Ezekiel.'

I called him in. The appearance of the low-minded cove was hailed with disapprobation from all sides, on account of his having brought his corkscrew with him. He pleaded 'the force of habit'.

'The force!' said Mrs. Sniff. 'Don't let us have you talking about force, for Gracious' sake. There! Do stand still where you are, with your back against the wall.'

He is a smiling piece of vacancy, and he smiled in the mean way in which he will even smile at the public if he gets a chance (language can say no meaner of him), and he stood upright near the door with the back of his head agin the wall, as if he was a waiting for somebody to come and measure his heighth for the Army.

'I should not enter, ladies,' says Our Missis, 'on the revolting disclosures I am about to make, if it was not in the hope that they will cause you to be yet more implacable in the exercise of the power you wield in a constitutional country, and yet more devoted to the constitutional motto which I see before me,' – it was behind her, but the words sounded better so, – '"May Albion never learn!"'

Here the pupils as had made the motto admired it, and cried, 'Hear! Hear! Hear!' Sniff, showing an inclination to join in chorus, got himself frowned down by every brow.

'The baseness of the French', pursued Our Missis, 'as displayed in the fawning nature of their Refreshmenting, equals, if not surpasses, anythink as was ever heard of the baseness of the celebrated Bonaparte.'

Miss Whiff, Miss Piff, and me, we drored a heavy breath, equal to saying, 'We thought as much!' Miss Whiff and Miss Piff seeming to object to my droring mine along with theirs, I drored another to aggravate 'em.

'Shall I be believed,' says Our Missis, with flashing eyes, 'when I tell you that no sooner had I set my foot upon that treacherous shore –'

Here Sniff, either bursting out mad, or thinking aloud, says, in a low voice: 'Feet. Plural, you know.'

The cowering that come upon him when he was spurned by all eyes, added to his being beneath contempt, was sufficient punishment for a cove so grovelling.

In the midst of a silence rendered more impressive by the turned-up female noses with which it was pervaded, Our Missis went on:

'Shall I be believed when I tell you, that no sooner had I landed,' this word with a killing look at Sniff, 'on that treacherous shore, than I was ushered into a Refreshment Room where there were – I do not exaggerate – actually eatable things to eat?'

A groan burst from the ladies. I not only did myself the honour of jining, but also of lengthening it out.

'Where there were,' Our Missis added, 'not only eatable things to eat, but also drinkable things to drink?'

A murmur, swelling almost into a scream, ariz. Miss Piff, trembling with indignation, called out, 'Name?'

'I *will* name,' said Our Missis. 'There was roast fowls, hot and cold; there was smoking roast veal surrounded with browned potatoes; there was hot soup with (again I ask shall I be credited?) nothing bitter in it, and no flour to choke off the consumer; there was a variety of cold dishes set off with jelly; there was salad; there was – mark me! – *fresh* pastry, and that of a light construction; there was a luscious show of fruit; there was bottles and decanters of sound small wine, of every size, and adapted to every pocket; the same odious statement will apply to brandy; and these were set out upon the counter so that all could help themselves.'

Our Missis's lips so quivered, that Mrs Sniff, though scarcely less convulsed than she were, got up and held the tumbler to them.

'This,' proceeds Our Missis, 'was my first unconstitutional experience. Well would it have been if it had been my last and worst. But no. As I proceeded farther into that enslaved and ignorant land, its aspect became more hideous. I need not explain to this assembly the ingredients and formation of the British Refreshment sangwich?'

Universal laughter, – except from Sniff, who, as sangwich-cutter, shook his head in a state of the utmost dejection as he stood with it agin the wall.

'Well!' said Our Missis, with dilated nostrils. 'Take a fresh, crisp, long, crusty penny loaf made of the whitest and best flour. Cut it longwise through the middle. Insert a fair and nicely fitting slice of ham. Tie a smart piece of ribbon round the middle of the whole to bind it together. Add at one end a neat wrapper of clean white paper by which to hold it. And the universal French Refreshment sangwich busts on your disgusted vision.'

A cry of 'Shame!' from all – except Sniff, which rubbed his stomach with a soothing hand.

'I need not,' said Our Missis, 'explain to this assembly the usual formation and fitting of the British Refreshment Room?'

No, no, and laughter. Sniff agin shaking his head in low spirits agin the wall.

'Well', said Our Missis, 'what would you say to a general decoration of everythink, to hangings (sometimes elegant), to easy velvet furniture, to abundance of little tables, to abundance of little seats, to brisk bright waiters, to great convenience, to a pervading cleanliness and tastefulness positively addressing the public, and making the Beast thinking itself worth the pains?'

Contemptuous fury on the part of all the ladies. Mrs. Sniff looking as if she wanted somebody to hold her, and everbody else looking as if they'd rayther not.

'Three times,' said Our Missis, working herself into a truly terrimenjious state, — 'three times did I see these shameful things, only between the coast and Paris, and not counting either: at Hazebroucke, at Arras, at Amiens. But worse remains. Tell me, what would you call a person who should propose in England that there should be kept, say at our own model Mugby Junction, pretty baskets, each holding an assorted cold lunch and dessert for one, each at a certain fixed price, and each within a passenger's power to take away, to empty in the carriage at perfect leisure, and to return at another station fifty or a hundred miles farther on?'

There was disagreement what such a person should be called. Whether revolutionise, atheist, Bright (*I* said him), or Un-English. Miss Piff screeched her shrill opinion last, in the words: 'A malignant maniac!'

'I adopt,' says Our Missis, 'the brand set upon such a person by the righteous indignation of my friend Miss Piff. A malignant maniac. Know, then, that that malignant maniac has sprung from the congenial soil of France, and that his malignant madness was in unchecked action on this same part of my journey.'

I noticed that Sniff was a-rubbing his hands, and that Mrs Sniff had got her eye upon him. But I did not take more particular notice, owing to the excited state in which the young ladies was, and to feeling myself called upon to keep it up with a howl.

'On my experience south of Paris,' said Our Missis, in a deep tone, 'I will not expatiate. Too loathsome were the task! But fancy this. Fancy a guard coming round, with the train at full speed, to inquire how many for dinner. Fancy his telegraphing forward the number of dinners. Fancy everyone expected, and the table elegantly laid for the complete party. Fancy a charming dinner, in a charming room, and the head-cook, concerned for the honour of every dish, superintending in his clean white jacket and cap. Fancy the Beast travelling six hundred miles on end, very fast, and with great punctuality, yet being taught to expect all this to be done for it!'

A spirited chorus of 'The Beast!'

I noticed that Sniff was agin a-rubbing his stomach with a soothing hand, and that he had drored up one leg. But agin I didn't take particular notice, looking on myself as called upon to stimulate public feeling. It being a lark besides.

'Putting everything together,' said Our Missis, 'French Refreshmenting comes to this, and oh, it comes to a nice total! First: eatable things to eat, and drinkable things to drink.'

A groan from the young ladies, kep' up by me.

'Second: convenience, and even elegance.'

Another groan from the young ladies, kep' up by me.

'Third: moderate charges.'

This time a groan from me, kep' up by the young ladies.

'Fourth: – and here,' says Our Missis, 'I claim your angriest sympathy, – attention, common civility, nay, even politeness!'

Me and the young ladies regularly raging mad all together.

'And I cannot in conclusion,' says Our Missis, with her spitefullest sneer, 'give you a completer pictur of that despicable nation (after what I have related), than assuring you that they wouldn't bear our constitutional ways and noble independence at Mugby Junction, for a single month, and that they would turn us to the right-about and put another system in our places, as soon as look at us; perhaps sooner, for I do not believe they have the good taste to care to look at us twice.'

The swelling tumult was arrested in its rise. Sniff, bore away by his servile disposition, had drored up his leg with a higher and a higher relish, and was now discovered to be waving his corkscrew over his head. It was at this moment that Mrs Sniff, who had kep' her eye upon him like the fabled obelisk, descended on her victim. Our Missis followed them both out, and cries was heard in the sawdust department.

You come into the Down Refreshment Room, at the Junction, making believe you don't know me, and I'll pint you out with my right thumb over my shoulder which is Our Missis, and which is Miss Whiff, and which is Miss Piff, and which is Mrs Sniff. But you won't get a chance to see Sniff, because he disappeared that night. Whether he perished, tore to pieces, I cannot say; but his corkscrew alone remains, to bear witness to the servility of his disposition.

Even before *Mugby Junction* Dickens had already written in comic terms about refreshments for railway travellers in *All the Year Round*, on 24 March 1860. Refreshments for the travelling public was a new idea in Britain, though not abroad, and had been stimulated by a parliamentary measure introduced by Gladstone earlier in 1860, so this piece is highly topical. He returns to the issue in a letter to his friend W. C. Macready, on 18 October 1869:

By the bye: At Elkington's I saw a pair of immense plated tea urns from a Railway station (Stafford) sent there to be repaired. They were honey-combed within in all directions, and had been supplying the passengers, under the active agency of hot water, with decomposed lead, copper, and a few other deadly poisons for Heaven knows how many years.

Refreshments for Travellers

In the late high winds I was blown to a great many places – and indeed, wind or no wind, I generally have extensive transactions on hand in the article of Air – but I have not been blown to any English place lately, and I very seldom have been blown to any English place in my life, where I could get anything good to eat and drink in five minutes, or where, if I sought it, I was received with a welcome.

This is a curious thing to consider. But before (stimulated by my own experiences and the representations of many fellow-travellers of every uncommercial and commercial degree) I consider it further, I must utter a passing word of wonder concerning high winds.

I wonder why metropolitan gales always blow so hard at Walworth. I cannot imagine what Walworth has done, to bring such windy punishment upon itself, as I never fail to find recorded in the newspapers when the wind has blown at all hard. Brixton seems to have something on its conscience; Peckham suffers more than a virtuous Peckham might be supposed to deserve; the howling neighbourhood of Deptford figures largely in the accounts of the ingenious gentlemen who are out in every wind that blows, and to whom it is an ill high wind that blows no good; but, there can hardly be any Walworth left by this time. It must surely be blown away. I have read of more chimney-stacks and house-copings coming down with terrific smashes at Walworth, and of more sacred edifices being nearly (not quite) blown out to sea from the same accursed locality, than I have read of practised thieves with the appearance and manners of gentlemen – a popular phenomenon which never existed on earth out of fiction and a police report. Again: I wonder why people are always blown into the Surrey Canal, and into no other piece of water? Why do people get up early and go out in groups, to be blown into the Surrey Canal? Do they say to one another, 'Welcome Death, so that we get into the newspapers'? Even that would be an insufficient explanation, because even then they might sometimes put themselves in the way of being blown into the Regent's Canal, instead of always saddling Surrey for the field. Some nameless policeman, too, is constantly, on the slightest provocation, getting himself blown into this same Surrey Canal. Will SIR RICHARD MAYNE see to it, and restrain that weak-minded and feeble-bodied constable?

To resume the consideration of the curious question of Refreshment. I am a Briton, and, as such, I am aware that I never will be a slave – and yet I have a latent suspicion that there must be some slavery of wrong custom in this matter. I travel by railroad. I start from home at seven or eight in the morning, after breakfasting hurriedly. What with skimming over the open landscape, what with mining in the damp bowels of the earth, what with banging booming and shrieking the scores of miles away, I am hungry when I arrive at the 'Refreshment' station where I am expected. Please to observe, expected. I have said, I am hungry; perhaps I might say, with greater point and force, that I am to some extent exhausted, and that I need – in the expressive French, sense of the word – to be restored. What is provided for my restoration? The apartment that is to restore me, is a wind-trap, cunningly set to inveigle all the draughts in that country-side, and to communicate a special intensity and velocity to them as they rotate in two hurricanes: one, about my wretched head: one, about my wretched legs. The training of the young ladies behind the counter who are to restore me, has been from their infancy directed

to the assumption of a defiant dramatic show that I am not expected.
It is in vain for me to represent to them by my humble and concilia-
tory manners, that I wish to be liberal. It is in vain for me to represent
to myself, for the encouragement of my sinking soul, that the young
ladies have a pecuniary interest in my arrival. Neither my reason nor
my feelings can make head against the cold glazed glare of eye with
which I am assured that I am not expected, and not wanted. The solitary man among the bottles would sometimes take pity on me, if he
dared, but he is powerless against the rights and mights of Woman.
(Of the page I make no account, for, he is a boy, and therefore the
natural enemy of Creation.) Chilling fast, in the deadly tornadoes
to which my upper and lower extremities are exposed, and subdued
by the moral disadvantage at which I stand, I turn my disconsolate
eyes on the refreshments that are to restore me. I find that I must
either scald my throat by insanely ladling into it, against time and
for no wager, brown hot water stiffened with flour; or, I must make
myself flaky and sick with Banbury cake; or, I must stuff into my
delicate organisation, a currant pincushion which I know will swell
into immeasurable dimensions when it has got there; or, must extort
from an iron-bound quarry, with a fork, as if I were farming an
inhospitable soil, some glutinous lumps of gristle and grease, called
pork-pie. While thus forlornly occupied, I find that the depressing
banquet on the table is, in every phase of its profoundly unsatisfactory character, so like the banquet at the meanest and shabbiest of
evening parties, that I begin to think I must have 'brought down'
to supper, the old lady unknown, blue with cold, who is setting her
teeth on edge with a cool orange, at my elbow – that the pastrycook
who has compounded for the company on the lowest terms per head,
is a fraudulent bankrupt, redeeming his contract with the stale stock
from his window – that, for some unexplained reason, the family
giving the party have become my mortal foes, and have given it on
purpose to affront me. Or, I fancy that I am 'breaking up' again,
at the evening conversazione at school, charged two-and-sixpence

in the half-year's bill; or breaking down again at that celebrated evening party given at Mrs Bogles's boarding-house when I was a boarder there, on which occasion Mrs Bogles was taken in execution by a branch of the legal profession who got in as the harp, and was removed (with the keys and subscribed capital) to a place of durance, half an hour prior to the commencement of the festivities.

Take another case. Mr Grazinglands, of the Midland Counties, came to London by railroad one morning last week, accompanied by the amiable and fascinating Mrs Grazinglands. Mr G. is a gentleman of a comfortable property, and had a little business to transact at the Bank of England, which required the concurrence and signature of Mrs G. Their business disposed of, Mr and Mrs Grazinglands viewed the Royal Exchange, and the exterior of St Paul's Cathedral. The spirits of Mrs. Grazinglands then gradually beginning to flag, Mr Grazinglands (who is the tenderest of husbands) remarked with sympathy, 'Arabella, my dear, I fear you are faint.'

Mrs Grazinglands replied, 'Alexander, I am rather faint; but don't mind me, I shall be better presently.'

Touched by the feminine meekness of this answer, Mr Grazinglands looked in at a pastrycook's window, hesitating as to the expediency of lunching at that establishment. He beheld nothing to eat, but butter in various forms, slightly charged with jam, and languidly frizzling over tepid water. Two ancient turtle-shells, on which was inscribed the legend, 'SOUPS,' decorated a glass partition within, enclosing a stuffy alcove, from which a ghastly mockery of a marriage-breakfast spread on a rickety table, warned the terrified traveller. An oblong box of stale and broken pastry at reduced prices, mounted on a stool, ornamented the doorway; and two high chairs that looked as if they were performing on stilts, embellished the counter. Over the whole, a young lady presided, whose gloomy haughtiness as she surveyed the street, announced a deep-seated grievance against society, and an implacable determination to be avenged. From a beetle-haunted kitchen below this

institution, fumes arose, suggestive of a class of soup which Mr
Grazinglands knew, from painful experience, enfeebles the mind,
distends the stomach, forces itself into the complexion, and tries
to ooze out at the eyes. As he decided against entering, and turned
away, Mrs Grazinglands, becoming perceptibly weaker, repeated,
'I am rather faint, Alexander, but don't mind me.' Urged to new
efforts by these words of resignation, Mr Grazinglands looked in at
a cold and floury baker's shop, where utilitarian buns unrelieved by
a currant consorted with hard biscuits, a stone filter of cold water, a
hard pale clock, and a hard little old woman with flaxen hair, of an
undeveloped-farinaceous aspect, as if she had been fed upon seeds.
He might have entered even here, but for the timely remembrance
coming upon him that Jairing's was but round the corner,

Now, Jairing's being an hotel for families and gentlemen, in
high repute among the midland counties, Mr Grazinglands plucked
up a great spirit when he told Mrs Grazinglands she should have
a chop there. That lady, likewise, felt that she was going to see
Life. Arriving on that gay and festive scene, they found the second
waiter, in a flabby undress, cleaning the windows of the empty
coffee-room, and the first waiter, denuded of his white tie, making
up his cruets behind the Post-office Directory. The latter (who took
them in hand) was greatly put out by their patronage, and showed
his mind to be troubled by a sense of the pressing necessity of
instantly smuggling Mrs Grazinglands into the obscurest corner of
the building. This slighted lady (who is the pride of her division of
the county) was immediately conveyed, by several dark passages,
and up and down several steps, into a penitential apartment at the
back of the house, where five invalided old plate-warmers leaned
up against one another under a discarded old melancholy sideboard,
and where the wintry leaves of all the dining-tables in the house
lay thick. Also, a sofa, of incomprehensible form regarded from
any sofane point of view, murmured 'Bed'; while an air of mingled
fluffiness and heeltaps, added, 'Second Waiter's'. Secreted in this

dismal hold, objects of a mysterious distrust and suspicion, Mr Grazinglands and his charming partner waited twenty minutes for the smoke (for it never came to a fire), twenty-five minutes for the sherry, half an hour for the table-cloth, forty minutes for the knives and forks, three-quarters of an hour for the chops, and an hour for the potatoes. On settling the little bill – which was not much more than the day's pay of a Lieutenant in the navy – Mr Grazinglands took heart to remonstrate against the general quality and cost of his reception. To whom the waiter replied, substantially, that Jairing's made it a merit to have accepted him on any terms; 'for,' added the waiter (unmistakably coughing at Mrs Grazinglands, the pride of her division of the county), 'when individuals is not staying in the 'Ouse, their favours is not as a rule looked upon as making it worth Mr Jairings's while; nor is it, indeed, a style of business Mr Jairing wishes.' Finally, Mr and Mrs Grazinglands passed out of Jairing's hotel for Families and Gentlemen, in a state of the greatest depression, scorned by the bar; and did not recover their self-respect for several days.

Or take another case.

Take your own case. You are going off by railway, from any Terminus. You have twenty minutes for dinner, before you go. You want your dinner, and, like Doctor Johnson, sir, you like to dine. You present to your mind, a picture of the refreshment-table at that terminus. The conventional shabby evening party supper – accepted as the model for all termini and all refreshment stations, because it is the last repast known to this state of existence of which any human creature would partake, but in the direst extremity – sickens your contemplation, and your words are these: 'I cannot dine on stale sponge-cakes that turn to sand in the mouth. I cannot dine on shining brown patties, composed of unknown animals within, and offering to my view the device of an indigestible star-fish in leaden pie-crust without. I cannot dine on a sandwich that has long been pining under an exhausted receiver. I cannot dine on barley-sugar.

I cannot dine on Toffee.' You repair to the nearest hotel, and arrive, agitated, in the coffee-room.

It is a most astonishing fact that the waiter is very cold to you. Account for it how you may, smooth it over how you will, you cannot deny that he is cold to you. He is not glad to see you, he does not want you, he would much rather you hadn't come. He opposes to your flushed condition, an immovable composure. As if this were not enough, another waiter, born, as it would seem, expressly to look at you in this passage of your life, stands at a little distance, with his napkin under his arm and his hands folded, looking at you with all his might. You impress on your waiter that you have ten minutes for dinner, and he proposes that you shall begin with a bit of fish which will be ready in twenty. That proposal declined, he suggests – as a neat originality – 'a weal or mutton cutlet'. You close with either cutlet, any cutlet, anything. He goes, leisurely, behind a door and calls down some unseen shaft. A ventriloquial dialogue ensues, tending finally to the effect that weal only, is available on the spur of the moment. You anxiously call out, 'Veal then!' Your waiter, having settled that point, returns to array your tablecloth, with a table napkin folded cocked-hat-wise (slowly, for something out of window engages his eye), a white wine-glass, a green wine-glass, a blue finger-glass, a tumbler, and a powerful field battery of fourteen castors with nothing in them; or at all events – which is enough for your purpose – with nothing in them that will come out. All this time, the other waiter looks at you – with an air of mental comparison and curiosity, now, as if it had occurred to him that you are rather like his brother. Half your time gone, and nothing come but the jug of ale and the bread, you implore your waiter to 'see after that cutlet, waiter; pray do!' He cannot go at once, for he is carrying in seventeen pounds of American cheese for you to finish with, and a small Landed Estate of celery and watercress. The other waiter changes his leg, and takes a new view of you doubtfully, now, as if he had rejected the resemblance to his brother, and had begun to think you more like his aunt or his grandmother. Again you beseech your waiter with pathetic indignation, to 'see after that cutlet!' He steps out to see after it, and by- and-by, when you are going away without it, comes back with it. Even then, he will not take the sham silver-cover off, without a pause for a flourish, and a look at the musty cutlet as if he were surprised to see it – which cannot possibly be the case, he must have seen it so often before. A sort of fur has been produced upon its surface by the cook's art, and, in a sham silver vessel stag-gering on two feet instead of three, is a cutaneous kind of sauce, of brown pimples and pickled cucumber. You order the bill, but your waiter cannot bring your bill yet, because he is bringing, instead, three flinty-hearted potatoes and two grim head of broccoli, like the occasional ornaments on area railings, badly boiled. You know that you will never come to this pass, any more than to the cheese and celery, and you imperatively demand your bill; but it takes time to get, even when gone for, because your waiter has to communicate with a lady who lives behind a sash-window in a corner, and who appears to have to refer to several Ledgers before she can make it out – as if you had been staying there a year. You become distracted to get away, and the other waiter, once more changing his leg, still looks at you but suspiciously, now, as if you had begun to remind him of the party who took the great-coats last winter. Your bill at last brought and paid, at the rate of sixpence a mouthful, your waiter reproachfully reminds you that 'attendance is not charged for a single meal,' and you have to search in all your pockets for sixpence more. He has a worse opinion of you than ever, when you have given it to him, and lets you out into the street with the air of one saying to himself, as you cannot doubt he is, ' I hope we shall never see you here again!'

Or, take any other of the numerous travelling instances in which, with more time at your disposal, you are, have been, or may be, equally ill served. Take the old-established Bull's Head with its old-established knife-boxes on its old-established sideboards, its old-established flue under its old-established four-post bed-steads in its old-established airless rooms, its old-established frouziness up-stairs and down stairs, its old-established cookery, and its old-established principles of plunder. Count up your injuries, in its side-dishes of ailing sweet-breads in white poultices, of apothecaries' powders in rice for curry, of pale stewed bits of calf ineffectually relying for an adventitious interest on forcemeat balls. You have had experience of the old-established Bull's Head's stringy fowls, with lower extremities like wooden legs, sticking up out of the dish; of its cannibalic boiled mutton, gushing horribly among its capers, when carved; of its little dishes of pastry – roofs of spermaceti ointment, erected over half an apple or four gooseberries. Well for you if you have yet forgotten the old-established Bull's Head's fruity port: whose reputation was gained solely by the old-established price the Bull's Head put upon it, and by the old-established air with which the Bull's Head set the glasses and D'Oyleys on, and held that Liquid Gout to the three-and-sixpenny wax-candle, as if its old- established colour hadn't come from the dyer's.

Or lastly, take to finish with, two cases that we all know, every day.

We all know the new hotel near the station, where it is always gusty, going up the lane which is always muddy, where we are sure to arrive at night, and where we make the gas start awfully when we open the front door. We all know the flooring of the passages and staircases that is too new, and the walls that are too new, and the house that is haunted by the ghost of mortar. We all know the doors that have cracked, and the cracked shutters through which we get a glimpse of the disconsolate moon. We all know the new people who have come to keep the new hotel, and who wish they had never come, and who (inevitable result) wish we had never come. We all know how much too scant and smooth and bright the new furniture is, and how it has never settled down, and cannot fit itself into right places, and will get into wrong places. We all know how the gas, being lighted, shows maps of Damp upon the walls. We all know how the ghost of mortar passes into our sandwich, stirs our negus, goes up to bed with us, ascends the pale bedroom chimney, and prevents the smoke from following. We all know how a leg of our chair comes off, at breakfast in the morning, and how the dejected waiter attributes the accident to a general greenness pervading the establishment, and informs us, in reply to a local inquiry, that he is thankful to say he is an entire stranger in that part of the country, and is going back to his own connexion on Saturday.

We all know, on the other hand, the great station hotel belonging to the company of proprietors, which has suddenly sprung up in the back outskirts of any place we like to name, and where we look out of our palatial windows, at little back yards and gardens, old summer-houses, fowl-houses, pigeon-traps, and pigsties. We all know this hotel in which we can get anything we want, after its kind, for money; but where nobody is glad to see us, or sorry to see us, or minds (our bill paid) whether we come, or go, or how, or when, or why, or cares about us. We all know this hotel, where we have no individuality, but put ourselves into the general post, as it were, and are sorted and disposed of according to our division. We all know that we can get on very well indeed at such a place, but still not perfectly well; and this may be, because the place is largely wholesale, and there is a lingering personal retail interest within us that asks to be satisfied.

To sum up. My uncommercial travelling has not yet brought me to the conclusion that we are close to perfection in these matters. And just as I do not believe that the end of the world will ever be near at hand, so long as any of the very tiresome and arrogant people who constantly predict that catastrophe are left in it, so, I shall have small faith in the Hotel Millennium, while any of the uncomfortable superstitions I have glanced at, remain in existence.

11

MANAGING THE RAILWAY

A. Gas Engine Supplying Motive Power.—B, Magneto Electric Machine.—C, D, E, F, Electric Current Indicators.—a, b, c, d, Contact Makers at the Ends of each Section.—e, f, g, h, Blocking Electro Magnets attached to each Section.—I, Blocking Electro-Magnet (Enlarged).—2, Contact Maker, as in Model.—3, Contact Maker as Required for Actual Use.—4, Map Indicator, Automatically Showing the Position of Trains on the Line.

PROFESSORS AYRTON AND PERRY'S NEW ELECTRIC RAILWAY

'Mrs Lirriper's Legacy', which was the Christmas story for 1864, published in *All the Year Round*, is a tale of Mrs Lirriper's adopted grandson Jemmy and one of her lodgers, Major Jackman, playing trains, but is used by Dickens to explore the whole range of issues involved in establishing the railway. He covers attitudes to the public, safety issues, investment, punctuality, all through the fanciful guise of the garrulous London landlady recounting her grandson's games to her friend.

From 'Mrs Lirriper's Legacy'

Ah! It's pleasant to drop into my own easy-chair my dear though a little palpitating what with trotting up-stairs and what with trotting down, and why kitchen stairs should all be corner stairs is for the builders to justify though I do not think they fully understand their trade and never did, else why the sameness and why not more conveniences and fewer draughts and likewise making a practice of laying the plaster on too thick I am well convinced which holds the damp, and as to chimney-pots putting them on by guess-work like hats at a party and no more knowing what their effect will be upon the smoke bless you than I do if so much, except that it will mostly be either to send it down your throat in a straight form or give it a twist before it goes there. And what I says speaking as I find of those new metal chimneys all manner of shapes (there's a row of 'em at Miss Wozenham's lodging-house lower down on the other side of the way) is that they only work your smoke into artificial patterns for you before you swallow it and that I'd quite as soon swallow mine plain, the flavour being the same, not to mention the conceit of putting up signs on the top of your house to show the forms in which you take your smoke into your inside.

Being here before your eyes my dear in my own easy-chair in my own quiet room in my own Lodging-House Number Eighty-one

Norfolk Street Strand London situated midway between the City and St. James's – if anything is where it used to be with these hotels calling themselves Limited but called unlimited by Major Jackman rising up everywhere and rising up into flagstaffs where they can't go any higher, but my mind of those monsters is give me a landlord's or landlady's wholesome face when I come off a journey and not a brass plate with an electrified number clicking out of it which it's not in nature can be glad to see me and to which I don't want to be hoisted like molasses at the Docks and left there telegraphing for help with the most ingenious instruments but quite in vain – being here my dear I have no call to mention that I am still in the Lodgings as a business hoping to die in the same and if agreeable to the clergy partly read over at Saint Clement's Danes and concluded in Hatfield churchyard when lying once again by my poor Lirriper ashes to ashes and dust to dust.

Neither should I tell you any news my dear in telling you that the Major is still a fixture in the Parlours quite as much so as the roof of the house, and that Jemmy is of boys the best and brightest and has ever had kept from him the cruel story of his poor pretty young mother Mrs Edson being deserted in the second floor and dying in my arms, fully believing that I am his born Gran and him an orphan, though what with engineering since he took a taste for it and him and the Major making Locomotives out of parasols broken iron pots and cotton-reels and them absolutely a getting off the line and falling over the table and injuring the passengers almost equal to the originals it really is quite wonderful.

And when I says to the Major, 'Major can't you by *any* means give us a communication with the guard?' the Major says quite huffy, 'No madam it's not to be done,' and when I says 'Why not?' the Major says, 'That is between us who are in the Railway Interest madam and our friend the Right Honourable Vice-President of the Board of Trade' and if you'll believe me my dear the Major wrote to Jemmy at school to consult him on the answer I should have before I could get even that amount of unsatisfactoriness out of the man, the reason being that when we first began with the little model and the working signals beautiful and perfect (being in general as wrong as the real) and when I says laughing 'What appointment am I to hold in this undertaking gentlemen?' Jemmy hugs me round the neck and tells me dancing, 'You shall be the Public Gran' and consequently they put upon me just as much as ever they like and I sit a growling in my easy-chair.

My dear whether it is that a grown man as clever as the Major cannot give half his heart and mind to anything – even a plaything – but must get into right down earnest with it, whether it is so or whether it is not so I do not undertake to say, but Jemmy is far out-done by the serious and believing ways of the Major in the management of the United Grand Junction Lirriper and Jackman Great Norfolk Parlour Line, 'For' says my Jemmy with the sparkling eyes when it was christened, 'we must have a whole mouthful of name Gran or our dear old Public' and there the young rogue kissed me, 'won't stump up'. So the Public took the shares – ten at ninepence, and immediately when that was spent twelve Preference at one and sixpence – and they were all signed by Jemmy and countersigned by the Major, and between ourselves much better worth the money than some shares I have paid for in my time. In the same holidays the line was made and worked and opened and ran excursions and had collisions and burst its boilers and all sorts of accidents and offences all most regular correct and pretty. The sense of responsibility entertained by the Major as a military style of station-master my dear starting the down train behind time and ringing one of those little bells that you buy with the little coal-scuttles off the tray round the man's neck in the street did him honour, but noticing the Major of a night when he is writing out his monthly report to Jemmy at school of the state of the Rolling Stock and the Permanent Way and all the rest of it (the whole kept upon the Major's sideboard and dusted with his own hands every morning before varnishing his boots) I notice him as full of thought and care as full can be and frowning in a fearful manner, but indeed the Major does nothing by halves as witness his great delight in going out surveying with Jemmy when he has Jemmy to go with, carrying a chain and a measuring-tape and driving I don't know what improvements right through Westminster Abbey and fully believed in the streets to be knocking everything upside down by Act of Parliament. As please Heaven will come to pass when Jemmy takes to that as a profession!

The essay 'Railway Strikes', published in *Household Words* on 11 January 1851, demonstrates Dickens's interest in contemporary issues and his enthusiasm for using his very popular weekly journal to raise important issues for debate. Railway strikes were rare during the early years of railway expansion, and this particular disagreement was settled without one. The widespread concern about railway safety at the time is also touched on. The 'MR GLYN' referred to by Dickens is George Glyn, later Baron Wolverton, the North-Western Railway's first chairman.

Railway Strikes

Everything that has a direct bearing on the prosperity, happiness, and reputation of the working-men of England should be a Household Word.

We offer a few remarks on a subject which has recently attracted their attention, and on which one particular and important branch of industry has made a demonstration, affecting, more or less, every other branch of industry, and the whole community; in the hope that there are few among the intelligent body of skilled mechanics who will suspect us of entertaining any other than friendly feelings towards them, or of regarding them with any sentiment but one of esteem and confidence.

The Engine Drivers and Firemen on the North Western line of Railway – the great iron high-road of the Kingdom, by which communication is maintained with Ireland, Scotland, Wales, the chief manufacturing towns of Great Britain, and the port which is the main artery of her commerce with the world – have threatened, for the second time, a simultaneous abandonment of their work; and relinquishment of their engagements with the Company they have contracted to serve.

We dismiss from consideration, the merits of the case. It would be easy, we conceive, to show, that the complaints of the men, even assuming them to be beyond dispute, were not, from the beginning of the manifestation, of a grave character, or by any mean hopeless of fair adjustment. But, we purposely dismiss that question. We purposely dismiss, also, the character of the Company, for careful, business-like, generous, and honourable management. We are content to assume that it stands no higher than the level of the very worst public servant bearing the name of railway, that the public possesses. We will suppose MR GLYN'S communications with the men, to have been characterised by overbearing evasion, and not (as they undoubtedly have been) by courtesy, good temper, self-command, and the perfect spirit of a gentleman. We will suppose the case of the Company to be the worst that such a case could be, in this country, and in these times. Even with such a reduction of it to its lowest possible point, and a corresponding elevation of the case of the skilled Railway servants to its highest, we must deny the moral right or justification of the latter to exert the immense power they accidentally possess, to the public detriment and danger.

We say, accidentally possess, because this power not been raised up by themselves. If there be ill-conditioned spirits among them who represent that it has been, they represent what is not true, and what a minute's rational consideration will show to be false. It is the result of a vast system of skilful combination, and a vast expenditure of wealth. The construction of the line, alone, against all the engineering difficulties it presented, involved an amount of outlay that was wonderful, even in England. To bring it to its present state of working efficiency, a thousand ingenious problems have been studied and solved, stupendous machines have been constructed, a variety of plans and schemes have been matured with incredible labour: a great whole has been pieced together by numerous capacities and appliances, and kept incessantly in motion. Even the character of the men, which stands deservedly high, has not been set up by themselves alone, but has been assisted by large contributions from these various sources. Without a good permanent way, and good engine power, they could not have established themselves in the public confidence as good drivers. Without good business-management in the complicated arrangements of trains for goods and passengers, they could not possibly have avoided accidents.

They have done their part manfully; but they could not have done it, without efficient aid in like manful sort, from every department of the great executive staff. And because it happens that the whole machine is dependent upon them in one important stage, and is delivered necessarily into their control – and because it happens that Railway accidents, when they do occur, are of a frightful nature, attended with horrible mutilation and loss of life and because such accidents, with the best precautions, probably must occur, in the event of their resignation in a body – is it, therefore, defensible to strike?

To that, the question comes. It is just so narrow, and no broader. We all know, perfectly well, that there would be no strike, but for the extent of the power possessed. Can such an exercise of it be defended, after due consideration, by any honest man?

We firmly believe that these are honest men – as honest men as the world can produce. But, we believe, also, that they have not well considered what it is that they do. They are laboriously and constantly employed; and it is the habit of many men, so engaged, to allow other men to think for them. These deputy- thinkers are not always the most judicious order of intellects. They are something quick at grievances. They drive Express Trains to that point, and Parliamentary to all other points. They are not always, perhaps, the best workmen, and are not so satisfied as the best workmen. They are, sometimes, not workmen at all, but designing persons, who have, for their own base purposes, immeshed the workmen in a system of tyranny and oppression. Through these, on the one hand, and through an imperfect or misguided view of the details of a case on the other, a strike (always supposing this great power in the strikers) may be easily set a going. Once begun, there is aroused a chivalrous spirit – much to be respected, however mistaken its manifestation – which forbids all reasoning. 'I will stand by my order, and do as the rest do. I never flinch from my fellow-workman. I should not have thought of this myself; but I wish to be true to the backbone, and here I put my name among the others.' Perhaps in no class of society, in any country, is this principle of honour so strong, as among most great bodies of English artisans.

But, there is a higher principle of honour yet; and it is that, we suggest to our friends the Engine Drivers and Firemen on the North Western Railway, which would lead to these greater considerations. First, what is my duty to the public, who are, after all, my chief employers? Secondly, what is my duty to my fellow workmen of all denominations: not only here, upon this Railway, but all over England?

We will suppose Engine Driver, John Safe, entering upon these considerations with his Fireman, Thomas Sparks. Sparks is one of the best of men, but he has a great belief in Caleb Coke, of Wolverhampton, and Coke says (because somebody else has said so, to him) 'Strike!'

'But, Sparks,' argues John Safe, sitting on the side of the tender, waiting for the Down Express, 'to look at it in these two ways, before we take any measures. Here we are, a body of men with a great public charge; hundreds and thousands of lives every day. Individuals among us may, of course, and of course do, every now and again give up their part of that charge, for one reason or another – and right too! But I'm not so sure that we can all turn our backs upon it at once, and do right.'

Thomas Sparks inquires 'Why not?'

'Why, it seems to me, Sparks,' says John Safe, 'rather a murdering mode of action.'

Sparks, to whom the question has never presented itself in this light, turns pale.

'You see,' John Safe pursues, 'when I first came upon this line, I didn't know –how could I? – where there was a bridge and where a tunnel where we took the turnpike road – where there was a cutting – where there was an embankment – where there was an incline – when full speed, when half, when slacken, when shut off, when your whistle going, when not. I got to know all such, by degrees; first, from them that was used to it; then, from my own use, Sparks.'

'So you did, John,' says Sparks.

'Well, Sparks! When we and all the rest that are used to it, Engine Drivers and Firemen all down the line and up again, lay our heads together, and say to the public, "If you don't back us up in what we want, we'll all go to the right-about, such a-day, so that nobody shall know all such" – that's rather a murdering mode of action, it appears to me.'

Thomas Sparks, still uncomfortably pale, wishes Coke of Wolverhampton were present, to reply.

'Because, it's saying to the public, "If you don't back us up, we'll do our united best towards your being run away with, and run into, and smashed, and jammed, and dislocated, and having your heads took off, and your bodies gleaned for, in small pieces and we hope you may!" Now, you know, that has a murdering appearance, Sparks, upon the whole!' says John Safe.

Sparks, much shocked, suggests that 'it mightn't happen.'

'True. But it might,' returns John Safe, 'and we know it might – no men better. We threaten that it might. Now, when we entered into this employment, Sparks, I doubt if it was any part of our fair bargain, that we should have a monopoly of this line, and a man-slaughtering sort of a power over the public. What do you think?'

Thomas Sparks thinks certainly not. But, Coke of Wolverhampton said, last Wednesday (as somebody else had said to him), that every man worthy of the name of Briton must stick up for his rights.

'There again!' says John Safe. 'To my mind, Sparks, it's not at all clear that any person's rights, can be another person's wrongs. And, that our strike must be a wrong to the persons we strike against, call 'em Company or Public, seems pretty plain.'

'What do they go and unite against us for, then?' demands Thomas Sparks.

'I don't know that they do,' replies John Safe. 'We took service with this company, as Individuals, ourselves, and not as a body; and you know very well we no more ever thought, then, of turning them off, as one man, than they ever thought of turning us off as one man. If the Company is a body, now, it was a body all the same when we came into its employment with our eyes wide open, Sparks.'

'Why do they make aggravating rules then, respecting the Locomotives?' demands Mr Sparks, 'which, Coke of Wolverhampton says, is Despotism!'

'Well, anyways they're made for the public safety, Sparks,' returns John Safe; 'and what's for the public safety, is for yours and mine. The first things to go, in a smash, is, generally, the Engine and Tender.'

'I don't want to be made more safe,' growls Thomas Sparks. 'I am safe enough, I am.'

'But, it don't signify a cinder whether you want it or don't want it,' returns his companion. 'You must be made safe, Sparks, whether you like or not, if not on your own account, on other people's.'

'Coke of Wolverhampton says, Justice! That's what Coke says!' observes Mr. Sparks, after a little deliberation.

'And a very good thing it is to say,' returns John Safe. 'A better thing to do. But, let's be sure we do it. I can't see that we good workmen do it to ourselves and families, by letting in bad un's that are out of employment. That's as to ourselves. I am sure we don't do it to the Company or Public, by conspiring together, to turn an accidental advantage against 'em. Look at other people! Gentlemen don't strike. Union doctors are bad enough paid (which we are not), but they don't strike. Many dispensary and hospital-doctors are not over well treated, but they don't strike, and leave the sick a groaning in their beds. So much for use of power. Then for taste. The respectable young men and women that serve in the shops, they didn't strike, when they wanted early closing.'

'All the world wasn't against them,' Thomas Sparks puts in.

'No; if it had been, a man might have begun to doubt their being in the right,' returns John Safe.

'Why, you don't doubt our being in the right, I hope?' says Sparks.

'If I do, I an't alone in it. You know there are scores and scores of us that, of their own accord, don't want no striking, nor anything of the kind.'

'Suppose we all agreed that we was a prey to despotism, what then?' asks Sparks.

'Why, even then, I should recommend our doing our work, true to the public, and appealing to the public feeling against the same,' replies John Safe. 'It would very soon act on the Company. As to the Company and the Public siding together against us, I don't find the Public too apt to go along with the Company when it can help it.'

'Don't we owe nothing to our order?' inquires Thomas Sparks.

'A good deal. And when we enter on a strike like this, we don't appear to me to pay it. We are rather of the upper sort of our order; and what we owe to other workmen, is, to set 'em a good example, and to represent them well. Now, there is, at present, a deal of general talk (here and there, with a good deal of truth in it) of combinations of capital, and one power and another, against workmen. I leave you to judge how it serves the workman's case, at such a time, to show a small body of his order, combined, in a misuse of power, against the whole community!'

It appears to us, not only that John Safe might reasonably urge these arguments and facts; but, that John Safe did actually present many of them, and not remotely suggest the rest, to the consideration of an aggregate meeting of the Engine Drivers and Firemen engaged on the Southern Division of the line, which was held at Camden Town on the day after Christmas Day. The sensible, moderate, and upright tone of some men who spoke at that meeting, as we find them reported in *The Times*, commands our admiration and respect, though it by no means surprises us. We would especially commend to the attention of our readers, the speech of an Engine Driver on the Great Western Railway, and the letter of the Enginemen and Firemen at the Bedford Station. Writing, in submission to the necessities of this publication immediately after that meeting was held, we are, of course, in ignorance of the issue of the question, though it will probably have transpired before the present number appears. It can, however, in no wise affect the observations we have made, or those with which we will conclude.

To the men, we would submit, that if they fail in adjusting the difference to their complete satisfaction, the failure will be principally their own fault, as inseparable, in a great measure, from the injudicious and unjustifiable threat into which the more sensible portion of them have allowed themselves to be betrayed. What the Directors might have conceded to temperate remonstrance, it is easy to understand they may deem it culpable weakness to yield to so alarming a combination against the public service and safety.

To the Public, we would submit, that the steadiness and patriotism of English workmen may, in the long run, be safely trusted; and that this mistake, once remedied, may be calmly dismissed. It is natural, in the first hot reception of such a menace, to write letters to newspapers, urging strong-handed legislation, or the enforcement of pains and penalties, past, present, or to come, on such deserters from their posts. But, it is not agreeable, on calmer reflection, to contemplate the English artisan as working under a curb or yoke, or even as being supposed to require one. His spirit is of the highest; his nature is of the best. He comes of a great race, and his character is famous in the world.

If a false step on the part of any man should be generously forgotten, it should be forgotten in him.

12

SUPPORTING THE
RAILWAY WORKERS

Dickens was always much in demand as a speaker on public occasions. In 1867 he was invited to speak at the ninth anniversary celebration of the foundation of the Railway Benevolent Institution, created to offer financial support for the widows and orphans of railway employees. This kind of philanthropic activity would have appealed to him greatly, as can be seen from the speech he delivered in London on 5 June at Willis's Rooms, King Street, St James's.

Speech to the Railway Benevolent Institution Annual Dinner, 1867

Although we have not yet left behind us by the distance of nearly fifty years the time when one of the first literary authorities of this country insisted upon the speed of the fastest railway train that the Legislature might disastrously sanction being limited by Act of Parliament to ten miles an hour, yet it does somehow happen that this evening, and every evening, there are railway trains running pretty smoothly to Ireland and to Scotland at the rate of fifty miles an hour; much as it was objected in its time to vaccination, that it must have a tendency to impart to human children something of the nature of the cow, whereas I believe to this very time vaccinated children are found to be as easily defined from calves as they ever were, and certainly they have no cheapening influence on the price of veal; much as it was objected that chloroform was a contravention of the will of Providence, because it lessened providentially-inflicted pain, which would be a reason for your not rubbing your face if you had the tooth-ache, or not rubbing your nose if it itched; so it was evidently predicted that the railway system, even if anything so absurd could be productive of any result, would infallibly throw half the nation out of employment; whereas, you observe that the very cause and occasion of our coming here together to-night is, apart from the various tributary channels of occupation which it has opened out, that it has called into existence a specially and directly employed population of upwards of 200,000 persons.

Now, gentlemen, it is pretty clear and obvious that upwards of 200,000 persons engaged upon the various railways of the United Kingdom cannot be rich; and although their duties require great care and great exactness, and although our lives are every day, humanly speaking, in the hands of many of them, still, for the most of these places there will be always great competition, because they are not posts which require skilled workmen to hold. Wages, as you know very well, cannot be high where competition is great, and you also know very well that railway directors, in the bargains they make, and the salaries which they pay, have to deal with the money of the shareholders, to whom they are accountable. Thus it necessarily happens that railway officers and servants are not remunerated on the whole by any means splendidly, and that they cannot hope in the ordinary course of things to do more than meet the ordinary wants and hazards of life. But it is to be observed that the general hazards are in their case, by reason of the dangerous nature of their avocations, exceptionally great, so very great, I find, as to be stateable, on the authority of a parliamentary paper, by the very startling round of figures, that whereas one railway traveller in 8,000,000 of passengers is killed, one railway servant in every 2,000 is killed.

Hence, from general, special, as well, no doubt, for the usual prudential and benevolent considerations, there came to be established among railway officers and servants, nine years ago, the Railway Benevolent Association. I may suppose, therefore, as it was established nine years ago, that this is the ninth occasion of publishing from this chair the banns between this institution and the public. Nevertheless, I feel bound individually to do my duty the same as if it had never been done before, and to ask whether there is any just cause or impediment why these two parties – the institution and the public – should not be joined together in holy charity. As I understand the society, its objects are five-fold – first, to guarantee annuities which, it is always to be observed, is paid out of the interest of invested capital, so that those annuities may be secure and safe – annual pensions, varying from £10 to £25, to distressed railway officers and servants incapacitated by age, sickness, or accident; secondly, to guarantee small pensions to distressed widows; thirdly, to educate and maintain orphan children; fourthly, to provide temporary relief for all those classes till lasting relief can be guaranteed out of funds sufficiently large for the purpose; lastly, to induce railway officers and servants to assure their lives in some well-established office by sub-dividing the payment of the premiums into small periodical sums, and also by granting a reversionary bonus of £10 per cent. on the amount assured from the funds of the institution.

This is the society we are met to assist – simple, sympathetic, practical, easy, sensible, unpretending. The number of its members is large, and rapidly on the increase: they number 12,000; the amount of invested capital is very nearly £15,000; it has done a world of good and a world of work in these first nine years of its life; and yet I am proud to say that the annual cost of the maintenance of the institution is no more than £250. And now if you do not know all about it in a small compass, either I do not know all about it myself, or the fault must be in my 'packing'.

One naturally passes from what the institution is and has done, to what it wants. Well, it wants to do more good, and it cannot possibly do more good until it has more money. It cannot safely, and therefore it cannot honourably, grant more pensions to deserving applicants until it grows richer, and it cannot grow rich enough for its laudable purpose by its own unaided self. The thing is absolutely impossible. The means of these railway officers and servants are far too limited. Even if they were helped to the utmost by the great railway companies, their means would still be too limited; even if they were helped – and I hope they shortly will be – by some of the great corporations of this country, whom railways have done so much to enrich. These railway officers and servants, on their road to a very humble and modest superannuation, can no more do without the help of the great public, than the great public, on their road from Torquay to Aberdeen, can do without them. Therefore, I desire to ask the public whether the servants of the great railways – who, in fact, are their servants, their ready, zealous, faithful, hard-working servants – whether they have not established, whether they do not every day establish, a reasonable claim to liberal remembrance.

Now, gentlemen, on this point of the case there is a story once told me by a friend of mine, which seems to my mind to have a certain application. My friend was an American sea-captain, and, therefore, it is quite unnecessary to say his story was quite true. He was captain and part owner of a large American merchant liner. On a certain voyage out, in exquisite summer weather, he had for cabin passengers one beautiful young lady, and ten more or less beautiful young gentlemen. Light winds or dead calms prevailing, the voyage was slow. They had made half their distance when the ten young gentlemen were all madly in love with the beautiful young lady. They had all proposed to her, and bloodshed among the rivals seemed imminent pending the young lady's decision. On this extremity the beautiful young lady confided in my friend the captain, who gave her discreet advice. He said: 'If your affections are disengaged, take that one of the young gentlemen whom you like the best and settle the question.' To this the beautiful young lady made reply, 'I cannot do that because I like them all equally well.' My friend, who was a man of resource, hit upon this ingenious expedient, said he, 'To-morrow morning at mid-day, when lunch is announced, do you plunge bodily overboard, head foremost. I will be alongside in a boat to rescue you, and take the one of the ten who rushes to your rescue, and then you can afterwards have him.' The beautiful young lady highly approved, and did accordingly. But after she plunged in, nine out of the ten more or less beautiful young gentlemen plunged in after her; and the tenth remained and shed tears, looking over the side of the vessel. They were all picked up, and restored dripping to the deck. The beautiful young lady upon seeing them said, 'What am I to do? See what a plight they are in. How can I possibly choose, because every one of them is equally wet?' Then said my friend the captain, acting upon a sudden inspiration, 'Take the dry one.' I am sorry to say that she did so, and they lived happy ever afterwards.

Now, gentlemen, in my application of this story, I exactly reverse my friend the captain's anecdote, and I entreat the public in looking about to consider who are fit subjects for their bounty, to give each his hand with something in it, and not award a dry hand to the industrious railway servant who is always at his back. And I would ask any one with a doubt upon this subject to consider what his experience of the railway servant is from the time of his departure to his arrival at his destination. I know what mine is. Here he is, in velveteen or in a policeman's dress, scaling cabs, storming carriages, finding lost articles by a sort of instinct, binding up lost umbrellas and walking sticks, wheeling trucks, counselling old ladies, with a wonderful interest in their affairs – mostly very complicated – and sticking labels upon all sorts of articles. I look around me – there he is again, in a station-master's uniform, directing and overseeing, with the head of a general, and the manners of a courteous host. There he is again in a guard's belt and buckle; with a handsome figure inspiring confidence in timid passengers. He is as gentle to the weak people as he is bold to the strong, and he has not a single hair in his beard that is not up to its work.

I glide out of the station, there he is again with his flags in his hands. There he is again in the open country, at a level crossing. There he is again at the entrance to the tunnel. At every station that I stop at, there he is again as alert as usual. There he is again at the arrival platform, getting me out of the carriage as if I was his only charge upon earth. Now, is there not something in the alacrity, in the ready zeal, in the interest of these men that is not acknowledged, that is not expressed in their mere wages? May it not be agreeable to the public to consider that this institution gives them the means of enjoying that something not only without compromise of their independence, but greatly to their permanent advantage? And if your experience coincides with mine, and enables you to have this good feeling for, and to say a good word in regard of, railway servants with whom we do come into contact, surely it may induce us to have some little sympathy with those whom – those signalmen for instance we rush past and do not distinctly see? And there are two sides to these points. If we take a human interest in them, will they not take a human interest in us? *(Cheers.)* We shall not be merely the 9.30 or the 10.30 rushing by, but we shall be an instalment of the considerate public that is ready to lend a hand to the poor fellows in the risk of their lives; and we cannot fail to derive a benefit from the interest they will consequently take in us.

I have, unconsciously, given you rather a long run, but I assure you that if you had done less on your part to get my steam up, I should have shut it off much sooner. Gentlemen, with a very hearty and real interest in the cause, and in the men, I beg you to drink 'Prosperity to the Railway Benevolent Institution'. *(Loud and prolonged cheering.)*

BIBLIOGRAPHY

Main extracts from Dickens's writings:

American Notes for General Circulation (1842), Chapter 4
The Life and Adventures of Martin Chuzzlewit (1843–4), from
    Chapter 21
Dealings with the Firm of Dombey and Son (1846–8), from
    Chapters 6, 15, 20 and 55

Items originally published in *Household Words:*

'The Individuality of Locomotives', Chip', 21 September 1850
'Railway Strikes', 11 January 1851
'A Narrative of Extraordinary Suffering', 12 July 1851
'A Flight', 30 August 1851
'Fire and Snow', 21 January 1854
'An Unsettled Neighbourhood', 11 November 1854
'The Lazy Tour of Two Idle Apprentices', with Wilkie Collins,
    October 1857

Items originally published in *All the Year Round:*

'Refreshments for Travellers', 24 March 1860
'The Calais Night Mail', 2 May 1863
'Mrs Lirriper's Legacy', Christmas story, December 1864
Mugby Junction ('Barbox Brothers', 'The Boy at Mugby', 'The Signal-Man'), Christmas story, December 1866

Extracts from *The Letters of Charles Dickens* (Pilgrim Edition, Oxford, volume 11):

to Thomas Mitton Tuesday, 13 June 1865
to W.W.F. de Cerjat, 30 November 1865

Speech given by Dickens to the Railway Benevolent Institution, 5 June 1867 (Fielding, K. J., ed. *The Speeches of Charles Dickens*, Harvester Press, 1988):

Other references are cited in the text.

Further reading

Histories of nineteenth-century Britain generally cover the major changes in transport during that time, including railways. Some suggestions for further reading, specifically on rail travel, are listed here. Most are fully illustrated.

Andrews, Cyril Bruyn, *The Railway Age*, Country Life, 1937

Carter, Ian, *Railways and Culture in Britain*, Manchester University Press, 2001

Dawson, Anthony, *Travelling on the Victorian Railway*, Amberley Publishing, 2017

Dawson, Anthony, *Working on the Victorian Railway*, Amberley Publishing, 2017

(both these books are very helpful on technical and engineering issues)

Freeman, Michael, *Railways and the Victorian Imagination*, Yale University Press, 1999

Morgan, Bryan (ed.) *The Railway-Lover's Companion*, Eyre and Spottiswoode, 1963 (a very comprehensive anthology of writing on railways in this period)

Ransom, P.J.G., *The Victorian Railway and How it Evolved*, Heinemann, 1990

Robbins, Michael, *The Railway Age*, Manchester University
    Press, 1998 (earlier editions from 1962 onwards)
Schivelsbusch, Wolfgang, *The Railway Journey*, Berg
    Publishing, 1977, paperback 1986
Thompson, Matt, *The Picturesque Railway*, History Press, 2015
    (highly recommended, fully-illustrated account of the
    lithographs of John Cooke Bourne)
Wolmar, Christian, *Fire and Steam*, Atlantic Books, 2007,
    paperback 2008

Readers who would prefer to approach the subject specifically
from a Dickens angle may find the following works of interest.

Allbutt, Robert, *Rambles in Dickens-Land*, Chapman and Hall,
    1899. This book provides railway itineraries for some of
    the early visitors to places with Dickens connections in
    the life and works.
Bentley, Nicholas, Slater, Michael and Burgis, Nina, *The
    Dickens Index*, Oxford University Press, 1990
Grossman, Jonathan H., *Charles Dickens's Networks: Public
    Transport and the Novel*, Oxford University Press, 2012.
    Grossman also contributed to Ledger and Furneaux,
    listed below.
House, Humphry, *The Dickens World*, Oxford University
    Press, 1941 (with a chapter on 'The Changing Scene')
Jordan, John, Patten, Robert L. and Catherine Waters (eds),
    The Oxford Handbook of Charles Dickens, Oxford
    University Press, 2018 (includes a chapter on
    technological change by Richard Menke)
Ledger, Sally and Furneaux, Holly (eds), *Charles Dickens in
    Context*, Cambridge University Press, 2011
Mengel, Ewald (ed.), *The Railway through Dickens's World*,
    Peter Lang, 1988 (provides an anthology of railways texts

originally published in Dickens's journals, but not – apart
from one – written by him)

Newlin, George (ed.) *Every Thing in Dickens*, Greenwood
Press, 1996 (contains a substantial anthology on
'Transport and Travel')

Sanders, Andrew, *Dickens and the Spirit of the Age*, Oxford
University Press, 1999 (includes a chapter on 'Signs of
the Times')

Sanders, Andrew, *Charles Dickens: Authors in Context*, Oxford
University Press, World's Classics series, 2003 (has a
section on 'Dickens and the Railway')

Schlicke, Paul (ed.), *The Oxford Reader's Companion to Dickens*,
Oxford University Press, 1999, paperback 2000 (includes
a full section on 'Transport')

Werner, Alex and Williams, Tony, *Dickens's Victorian London*,
Ebury Press, 2011. Published to accompany the Museum
of London's Dickens Bi-Centenary exhibition, it includes
a section on 'Railways and Construction', with many
photographs of changes brought about by the railways.

Useful contact details

The Dickens Fellowship is a worldwide organisation of enthusiasts for the life, works and times of Charles Dickens, with a journal, *The Dickensian*, published three times a year. www.dickensfellowship.org

The Charles Dickens Museum. In 1922, the Fellowship purchased 48 Doughty Street, a Georgian terraced house in Bloomsbury and home of Charles Dickens from 1837 to 1839. In 1925 the house was opened to the public as the Dickens House Museum, and is now known as the Charles Dickens Museum. www.dickensmuseum.com

Dickens Journals Online provides a complete, free-access set of Dickens's journals, *Household Words* and *All the Year Round*. www.djo.org